Right Place at the Write Time

A COLORFUL AND CANDID BEHIND-THE-SCENES LOOK AT
MY 60 YEARS IN THE RECORDING INDUSTRY

A Memoir

D. Bergen White

WITH MITCHELL B. WHITE

Right Place at the Write Time Copyright © 2021 by D. Bergen White.
All rights reserved. Printed in the United States of America.
ISBN 978-0-578-33210-9

Disclaimers

I'm a musician and an arranger. I've been writing music since the early sixties, but by no means do I consider myself a literary writer. Therefore, the stories that follow are simply as I remember them. I'm sharing them as if I was speaking with you, and perhaps we can relive the moments together.

As you may notice, many of the photos are in strange shapes. The reason is these are photos that I have trimmed to fit into collages I have all over my walls at home. If I had known I was going to write a book, I would not have chopped them up so much. There are also many digital photos coming from various sources and varying quality. I apologize for that but hope the image adds to the story. Looking back, I wish I'd taken even more photos, they bring back the greatest memories.

If you read this book cover to cover you will notice there is some repetition and overlap. This is intentional so that someone with a shorter attention span can read any section they like and the story will be complete.

My family urged me for years to write this book but I just kept putting it off thinking maybe I'll do it later. One day my dear friend Conni Ellisor (a marvelous violinist and also my present contractor for strings), suggested that she would love to be my biographer. She and I fiddled (no pun intended) with it for a while until we hit some snags and everything was put on pause until my third son, Mitch stepped in and literally took over. If you look in the dictionary for "technologically challenged" you will find a picture of me. In spite of my dreadful ignorance on the computer or anything that requires at least a little skill in those areas, Mitch just kept urging me on. Many times painstakingly urging me on. Everything from how I was trying to tell these stories to the pics that are included, hardbacks or paperbacks and everything else, Mitch was guiding me through it. Simply stated, this book would never have happened without Mitch!

Table of Contents

The Beginning — 1
    Chapters 1–6

The Producers — 22
    Chapters 7–41

The Arists and Writers — 104
    Chapters 42–99

The Musicians — 215
    Chapters 100–124

The Singers — 258
    Chapters 125–137

The Rest — 281
    Chapters 138–145

Foreword

Imagine growing up with a dad who was quiet, humble, soft spoken, and always there when you needed him. Now imagine reading a book where you find out your 'normal' dad is a world renown hero and responsible for some of the greatest acts in mankind's history. That is EXACTLY how I felt after reading Bergen's memoirs. I HAD NO IDEA! And I have known Bergen for years and work with him every day!!

You are going to LOVE the stories that fill these pages, and you are going to see Bergen is the common thread that runs through some of the most popular recordings in history. If I would have known what I know now about Bergen before I met him, I'm not sure I could have found the words to say, "Hello." But his humble approach as a fellow musician and human being, makes you feel so at ease when you meet him. He has that same 'gift' in this book. From Elvis to the Super Bowl, you will find yourself immersed in some of the biggest moments in entertainment history, but it is in the personal stories where you will simply find yourself. A man raised like all of us, the stories and lessons in this book will lead you to the revelation that the rarest moments in history are created by everyday people.

As a musician, I am embarrassed I did not know the history of Bergen White…as a friend, I am proud. But what I loved most and what I took away from this book is what makes a person's amazing accomplishments shine even brighter is that same person's humility. I love Bergen White.

—GARTH BROOKS

Right Place at the Write Time

1

In the Beginning

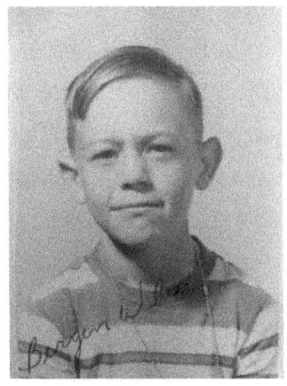

Me at age 8 in Seminole, Texas (already an asshole).

I was born on July 18, 1939, in Miami, Oklahoma (pronounced *My-am-ee* in Florida, *My-am-uh* in Oklahoma). My father, Dee Wayne White, was a minister of music, and every year or so he would feel God was leading him to a different Southern Baptist church, so we moved a lot. I spent my first six years in Joplin, Missouri, where my dad did his music thing but was also employed at Atlas Powder plant where they manufactured ammunition for World War II. My main memory from Joplin is when my mom and dad, and older sister, Barbara, and I sat in the living room in front of a big Zenith radio that was taller than I was, listening to the atomic bomb being dropped on Hiroshima in 1945.

After Joplin we went to Neosho, Missouri, then Shawnee, Oklahoma, where my dad attended Oklahoma Baptist University and did his music at First Baptist Church in Tecumseh. My unpleasant memories of Tecumseh all stem from the pastor, Loren Messenger, who would sit in his chair in front of the entire congregation and clean his ears with a bobby pin while the music was going on. I was too young and stupid to realize how disgusting that was. He and my dad used to tease me by accusing me of "peering out the window," "hesitating on the doorstep," and the worst of all, "slumbering in my sleep". I would shout, "I DID NOT!" I was getting so frustrated I would be in tears. They thought it was hilarious. I did not!

Next we went to Seminole, Texas, when I was about eight, then Memphis, where I was first chair trombone in the Humes High School band, even though I was only in the seventh grade. For those who might remember, Humes High was the same school Elvis attended. He was there about five years before me, but enough about Elvis.

When I was twelve we moved to Nashville. I attended eighth grade at Woodmont Elementary School, then went to Hillsboro High, followed by Belmont College, where my dad was the chairman of the division of Fine Arts. Through all my early years, with all the moving and such, I never remember a time when I was not singing in my dad's choirs at church every Sunday, every service. I hated it since all my buddies were sitting in the congregation giggling while I had to sing in the choir, but even then, I was learning.

For instance, somewhere in there I learned to read music. I didn't think it was a big deal, I thought everyone did that. I remember around the age of eight or nine singing in Handel's "Messiah" and Mendelssohn's "Elijah". About the same time, I was diggin' on "Come On-a My House" by Rosemary Clooney. It was the first time I ever took notice of a harpsichord.

At Belmont College (which would later become Belmont University), my dad had a male glee club, a female glee club, a modern quartet where we'd sing the Four Freshmen's and Hi-Lo's stuff, and also a goofy barbershop quartet that I hated. I thought it was the stupidest shit I'd ever heard, and still do, but of course I had to be in both quartets and the male glee club, where I sang and played a bass fiddle, which I taught myself to play. Looking back I'm surprised my dad hadn't figured out a way to have me in the female glee club.

Dad would pick Four Freshmen records like "I'll Be Seeing You" and tell me to transcribe the parts so we could sing them in concerts. At the same time, I had no idea how that was preparing me for what would later become my career. I've got to say that at no time did I ever think I would wind up in the music business. I was determined to play professional baseball, and to be quite honest, I was pretty damn good. Good enough that three major league teams were scouting me. I was playing shortstop at the time, and they all agreed I was out of position. They said I had the range for shortstop but not a strong enough arm to make the throw from the hole to first and thought I should be at third or second base. But after getting beaned (being hit in the head with a ninety-five mile-per-hour fastball—while my sweet mama was watching) I decided the diamond was not for me.

I've got to say something here about my mother, who was always there for me. Her maiden name was Carman June Bergen, and she was the daughter of Clarence Elmore Bergen, who was a Baptist minister, and my maternal grandmother, Nell. They lived in Picher, Oklahoma, once a boom town for zinc mining. The town has now been condemned due to the poisoning of the land from the mining that went on there for years. The population of Picher today is zero. My sister, Barbara, and I used to spend our summers in Picher, never aware that it might be dangerous to be there. Maybe that explains what's wrong with me now!

My sister was a marvelous pianist, an accompanist who could sit down at a piano and play anything you stuck in front of her. She was such a great accompanist because you never noticed her. My dad used to say if you notice the accompanist, it probably meant they were playing too much, taking attention away from the singer. I, on the other hand, played everything by ear. It used to really piss off my sister when I would sit down and play something we'd just heard on the radio using only three fingers on my right hand, one on my left.

Anyway, in all those different towns we lived in my mama was always singing alto in my dad's choirs. She always supported my dad and I even when we were making mistakes, which was quite often for me. I guess just like everyone's mama, she was very special. We lost her in 2000, and I miss her every day.

Here's a story about my mama that will tell you a little more about her, and I guess about me too. My sister's boyfriend at Belmont College was named Parker Holder (he would later become her husband). I always teased him and called him "Pecker Holder". Hell, that's funny just to say it. He is a really great guy and was a wonderful husband to my sister. Anyway, my precious mama was as naïve as she was sweet, and one night we're having a glee club party at our home. The guests were all arriving, and when Parker walked in, Mama playfully said, "Well, there's Pecker. It's so good to see you Mr. Pecker Holder." Well, everyone was giggling, so I pulled Mama into a different room and explained why everyone was laughing. Let me tell you, if looks could kill I would've died instantly! She gave me a look that I'd never seen from my mama before, and she hardly came out of that room the rest of the night. Only my mama would forgive me for that.

My dad grew up in Baxter Springs, Kansas, which was also a mining town. His parents were Ed and Maude, and he had five brothers, three of which worked in the zinc mines in that area. My dad lost one of his brothers, David, when he fell into a mine shaft at age eleven. Homer was a traveling musician who died in Arizona at an early age from a combination of tuberculosis and syphilis. Thank God my dad escaped that life.

In the late '30s to early '40s, Dad sang and played fiddle in his own traveling band, sort of a western swing band I suppose, called "Flash White and the Flickers". If I had been alive then, I would've surely been a Flicker. Dad also was in the Air Force in World War II as a radio operator.

In The Beginning

Mom and Dad singing at a funeral circa 1947.

Me and my sister Barbara, the first person to call me an asshole circa 1941.

2

Belmont College

(For those of you who don't give a rat's ass about my college experience, you can kindly skip this chapter.)

Belmont College would later become Belmont University, but when I went there in 1958 it was still a college and previously had been an all-girls school called Ward-Belmont. It had maybe four hundred students on a good day. I did everything at Belmont but study, and was pretty much kept in school only because my father was the chairman of the Division of Fine Arts and was adept at begging.

Also, my father was the founder of the music program at Belmont. You will never hear his name mentioned but if you've followed "Christmas at Belmont" and seen all the different groups that perform, all of that started with my father. Many have been given and accepted credit for it, like Bob Malloy, but all they did was imitate my father. Anyway, just wanted to get that off my chest.

As I mentioned earlier, I was in the male glee club, the modern quartet, the yucky, embarrassing barbershop quartet, and played on the baseball team. I was captain of the team my senior year when we went to the Volunteer State Athletic Conference Championship series against

Mighty Carson Newman. We won the first game but lost the next two, and the championship.

As fate would have it, the baseball tournament was at the exact same time as the Glee Club Spring Tour, so just as soon as the tournament ended I flew to Houston to join the glee club, which was already halfway through the tour. My father was very upset that I had missed part of the glee club tour (even though there were 32 members of the glee club and there were only 11 players on the baseball team!), so upset in fact that he was not speaking to me. As you might imagine, the rest of that tour was not much fun.

This next story is about one of my many antics at Belmont. There was this bell in the tower above Acklen Hall on campus that we called the "forbidden bell" since there was a steadfast rule that no one touch that bell. It had been there since the Civil War and naturally, if the bell was forbidden, we just had to ring it, right? But the stairs leading up to the bell were roped off, and the door was locked like Fort Knox. No way we could get to the bell? Wrong! Jesse Cabler, Herman Knox, Boots Kirby and I were determined to ring that bell, which hadn't been rung in probably a hundred years. I can't remember how we did it, but we figured out a way to get around all the safeguards to reach the "forbidden bell."

The next part was easy... so we thought. We had purchased a ball of heavy twine that we attached to the bell, then we threw the ball of twine out of the tower to the ground. We snuck it back to the boys' dorm, where we anxiously awaited the bewitching hour for the forbidden ringing.

Midnight struck and we were giggling as we pulled the twine. The bell didn't ring, so we kept pulling the twine until the broken end came through the window. In our exuberance to ring the bell we did not consider the fact the bell weighed probably five hundred pounds and our ball of twine was not sufficient to the task. It would've taken a two-inch chain to do it, so we were thwarted in our foolhearty attempt to ring the "forbidden bell." Oh well.

I was fortunate to get to play baseball at Belmont with some marvelous athletes and friends. Boots Kirby, Charlie Fentress, Tommy Frensley, Ray Hogan, Herman Knox, Jesse Cabler, and Jerry Vradenburg were my teammates, and we are still close friends to this day, although a few have passed away. I mentioned earlier about getting "beaned". Well, Jerry Vradenburg was the pitcher who hit me in the left temple with his fastball when we were playing against each other in the summer league. After a short hospital stay, then a few weeks in bed at home, Jerry came by the house selling "funeral insurance." All the guys thought it was really funny. My mother did not.

Tommy Frensley had a dry wit that people either loved or found a bit offensive. Our baseball coach, Harold "Buster" Boguski, was an ex-major leaguer who took his job very seriously. He had played with the New York Giants long before they moved to San Francisco. Anyway, he and Tommy clashed, to say the least. We weren't having a very good season and there was a lot of unrest, pointing fingers, grumbling going on, so "Bo" — we called him "Bo" — scheduled a team meeting to try to clear the air. We were all sitting around home plate while Bo lectured us about taking the game a little more seriously.

I've got to mention that Bo invented the "southern twang." Instead of "swing the bat," it was *"swang* the bat*"*. Instead of "hell," it was *"hail"*. Bo said instead of bitching all the time, if we had any suggestions, he wanted to hear them, so immediately Tommy spoke up. "I think we need to run more, Bo. Steal some bases and take advantage of our speed." Bo answered, "Well, *hail*, Tommy, we can't steal first base!" Everyone but Tommy thought that was really funny.

Another Tommy and Bo incident… we were playing Union University in Jackson, Tennessee. They had a sure-fire major league prospect that was pitching against us. It was getting late in the game when Tommy came to bat with runners in scoring position. The first two pitches were like rockets across the plate that Tommy just sneared at. Two strikes, no balls when Bo shouted from his third-base coaching position, *"Hail,* Tommy, you've gotta *swang* the bat!" The next pitch looked like it was high and inside but wound up low and over the outside corner. Before the umpire could call Tommy out, Tommy shouted, "Strike three and a beauty!" Tommy was replaced in left field.

Ray Hogan pitched for this bunch and had a very short fuse for all the foolishness the rest of us really enjoyed. One day when we were playing Western Kentucky we were throwing the ball around the infield whilst Ray was waiting on the mound and one of us hit him in the back of the head. Ray just shook his head as he walked off the mound mumbling, "I've gotta get outta here before these dipshits kill me!"

Charlie Fentress saved my life over and over, since I was always pissing off opposing players. Charlie, Tommy, Boots, and I were playing basketball in this winter league for Jackson Realty, and this big guy playing for Ball State named Russ Wingo kept knocking me out of the way when I was trying to get in position to get a rebound. This happened over and over until finally I tripped him, as we were running back up the court. We fell on the floor together; Russ had one hand on my head while the other was cocked to hit me when Charlie grabbed Russ and said, "Don't hit him, Russ, he didn't mean to do it." Russ screamed that I certainly did mean to do it. Charlie continued to hold Russ and said to me, "Bergen, did you mean to trip Russ?" Naturally I said, "Of course not, Charlie". Ha-ha!

One night Charlie and I walked down to the Hillsboro Diner to have a few libations, which was forbidden at Belmont College. A few turned out to be way too many. We were walking back to Belmont highly inebriated, singing "Lonely Street" when Charlie realized he was singing alone, looked back, and saw my feet sticking out of a hedge. Ole Bergy had not yet discovered how to hold his liquor.

One more Charlie story: W. C. Griffith was the Athletic Director at Belmont and had been a prize fighter when he was in the military, so he taught boxing. Charlie was one of his students. One day as Charlie and Mr. Griffith were sparring in front of the class, Mr. Griffith stopped and told Charlie to hit him in the stomach. He said, "C'mon, Charlie, hit me in the stomach, you can't hurt me. Hit me hard. You can't hurt me." Charlie said, "I don't want to hit you, Mr. Griffith," but Mr. Griffith insisted, so Charlie hit him in the stomach. Mr. Griffith had to be carried into the training room and could hardly speak for three hours, but Charlie got an A.

Mr. Griffith was also the director of intramural sports. Belmont had a basketball and a baseball team but no football team, so we played intramural flag football. Basically in flag football, you try to pull the flag out of the back of the player's pants to get him down, but if that doesn't work you are allowed to brutally mug him. Griff was officiating this championship game when a pass was thrown to me in the open field. I leapt to catch it but was hit hard and landed awkwardly on my left shoulder and broke my left collar bone. Griff sent an assistant into the locker room to get some rolls of gauze and tape and said, "*Hyere*"—(his word for here)—"this will be a good learning experience so *hyere*, hand me that gauze." Griff started wrapping gauze and tape around me to support my left shoulder. In a few minutes I looked like a mummy, and when I stood up my right shoulder was in place but my left shoulder was hanging loosely toward the ground. One of the players said, "Mr. Griffith, looks like you taped the wrong shoulder," and Griff responded, "Well *hyere*, now it's time to get him to the hospital." A great learning experience it was.

On a frigid winter morning the class had gathered wearing heavy coats since Griff kept the classroom so cold. Griff strutted in with a short-sleeve shirt on and admonished all of us for being such "pansies". He described his breakfast, which was a bowl of his favorite serails (his word for cereal) and some concentrated prune juice. "*Hyere*, that's the way to start the day," he said. He started reading from a book and about ten minutes in he stopped, walked over to the window, opened it wide, clapped his hands, and said, "Oh, what a beautiful morning." It was ten degrees and overcast with about a twenty-five mile-an-hour wind with gusts up to thirty-five. The wind blew the pages in the book he was reading about fifty pages over, then Griff walked back to his desk and continued reading as if nothing had happened. We didn't learn a hell of a lot from Mr. Griffith.

Boots, Charlie, Vradenburg, and I all played baseball together for Nashville Sporting Goods in the city league and won several regional championships. Sometime around '61 or '62 we played the Falstaff Brewers for the championship in Chattanooga at Engle Stadium. Falstaff had a few ex-major leaguers who didn't quite know how to react to Boots and I standing on our dugout steps singing a little tune I had written for the occasion that went like this: "We're for you all the way, Falstaff Brewers, but for you all the way is second place. You'se lucky on the draw but you cannot win 'em all, go on to second place, Falstaff Brewers." ("lucky on the draw" meant Falstaff wouldn't have even been in the tournament had they not drawn the lucky straw.) For this particular performance Boots brought his guitar and I brought my bass fiddle. Both dugouts were laughing as well as many people in the stands. I'm not positive, but I think we won.

Jerry, Boots, and Charlie were all inducted into the Tennessee Amateur Baseball Hall of Fame. Due to an egregious error in judgement, I was not. Maybe the bass fiddle was out of tune.

Jerry went on to coach the Gallatin High Basketball team to the State Championship. Charlie went on to become the fire chief in West Nashville. Tommy went on to coach the Hillsboro High basketball team to the State Finals two years in a row and was honored by having the basketball floor named after him.

Boots and I just went on.

3

Post-Belmont

After graduating Belmont in 1962, I had no idea what I was gonna do and was afraid I was gonna get drafted into the Vietnam War, so Boots Kirby suggested I teach school since teachers weren't getting drafted. Luckily I just happened to have enough credits to get a temporary teaching certificate so I taught math and science to 7th and 8th graders at Fairview Elementary School. What a joke! I was a pathetic math student and an even more pathetic teacher, but my students thought I was funny so I got away with it.

The science was a bigger joke. All I really did was try to find interesting experiments to do with the kids. One of them was finding out what happens to plants in the absence of light. I can't remember what that's called, but it seemed so easy so I asked several of the students to bring in some nice healthy green plants, explaining that we would put them in a closet and see what happened over a certain period of time. What could possibly go wrong? Naturally I forgot about it, and so did the students. So when the school year ended and the kids were off for the summer, I was cleaning up my classroom, when I opened the closet door, and there they were... dead as a doornail. What an experiment!

One day I'd gone to the teachers' lounge to relax and read the newspaper when Boots walked in. He didn't feel very good after a late night of eating raw oysters and drinking way too much beer. We talked for a few minutes and when he stood up and looked out the window of the door, he saw this real cutie fourth-grade teacher coming toward the lounge. He proceeded to "cut the cheese", "break some wind", "cut a fart", whatever you want to call it, but it turned the air a blueish-green color and then he went out the back door. So there I sat reading the newspaper, and exactly when the fart reached me this cutie prissed into the lounge and looked at me in horror. What was I gonna say since I was the only person in there? "Hey, it wasn't me! I didn't do it"? She fled the scene of the crime, and I found Boots sitting in the middle of the basketball court with tears streaming down his face from laughter. He does that a lot; when he laughs, he cries.

Near the end of my second year teaching, a friend I'd had since the eighth grade, Bobby Russell, was already in the music business and had become a great songwriter ("Honey", "Little Green Apples", "The Night the Lights Went Out in Georgia", to name a few). He called asking if I wanted make a little extra money singing harmony on copies of this new group called the Beatles. Bobby was also an excellent singer and was singing "sound-a-likes" (the record company would pick the fastest moving records in Billboard and Cashbox magazines, hire a band and orchestra and singers to "copy" the record, then sell them for 39 cents on racks in department stores). I agreed, since I was making a whopping $330 a month teaching. THAT was the beginning of my music business career.

I sang on these for a while, until one day the producer, William Beasley, asked me if I wanted to try arranging some of these copies. I thought, why not? The first one I did was "Yesterday" by the Beatles. I was scared to death standing in front of the string quartet: Brenton Banks and Howard Carpenter on violin, Lillian Hunt on viola, and Byron Bach on cello, along with Wayne Moss on acoustic guitar. We ran through it one time and then Lillian Hunt whispered, "Bergen, could you step over here?" I thought, oh shit! I stumbled over to her and she whispered again, "Bergen, I can't play that note," pointing to the note with her bow. I asked, "Why not? You don't like it?" She answered, "It's not on the instrument." "Well," I said, "how low can you go?" She said a C was the lowest note on the viola. That went straight into my brain and I didn't make that particular mistake again. That was the way I learned most all the ranges on instruments.

I've got to admit I never understood why all the horns had to be in different keys. What asshole decided that? Trumpets up a step, trombones are concert, tenor sax is a ninth up, flutes are concert, French horns up a fifth. What kind of insane shit is that? Thank God Bill Justis came into my life and became my mentor; he taught me so much about arranging. He was actually doing all the arranging on the sound-a-likes himself when I started, but he was so busy doing films and writing charts for Frank Sinatra, Dean Martin, and Sammy Davis Jr. that he was glad to turn the gig over to me.

Bill had hired me when I first got into the business and taught me to do lead sheets in his office called "Tunesville" on 17th Avenue South in Nashville, next to RCA Recording Studios. I'd be sitting in my office trying to arrange one of these things when I would hear an instrument on the recording and not have a clue what it was. I'd tap on Bill's door and no matter what he was doing he would stop to help me out. I'd put on a 45 and say, "What the hell is that?"

I've got to explain here that Bill was the original "jive cat." He'd say, "Hey, man, that's an English horn, man." I'd say, "How do you write for an English horn?" He would explain it to me, and yes, the English horn is another weird one, up a fifth, like the French horn. Yikes! I'd never had an orchestration class of any kind, but if you think about it, what better way to learn arranging than to copy "hit" records. That is what I was doing. I was being paid to learn to arrange. Crazy, I tell ya.

4

The Nashville Cats

Around 2000, the Country Music Hall of Fame created an award that instead of honoring the artist, would honor the side musicians, producers, arrangers, and engineers who helped create the "hit" recordings. On June 15, 2013, I was given this distinction and was allowed to join a very select group of creative honorees. Researcher Abi Tapia found out things about me that I didn't know myself, then Bill Lloyd conducted the interview.

The interview lasted about an hour and a half, then was followed by me signing autographs on my "Nashville Cats" poster. The waiting line for my autograph was extremely long since I have a very large family. You can easily find my autographed "Nashville Cats" poster hanging over the toilet in the green room restroom of the Ford Theatre at the Country Music Hall of Fame. I was so proud to have my entire family sitting in the front row at the presentation. Many thanks to the Country Music Association and Hall of Fame, as I feel extremely honored and blessed to be a member of the "Nashville Cats".

In the green room after my induction in 2013.

(L to R: Chip Young, Wayne Moss, Weldon Myrick, Hargis "Pig" Robbins, Jerry Kennedy, Me, Fred Foster, Millie Kirkham, Reggie Young, David Briggs, Ray Stevens and Bill Lloyd, crouching)

5

The "Breakfast Club"

The "Breakfast Club" has been gathering for breakfast every Saturday morning for quite some time. Norro Wilson, after much persuasion, talked me into giving it a try about ten years ago, and until COVID struck in 2020, I've hardly ever missed breakfast at LePeep on Harding Road. A lot of us call it "LePoop" for reasons I'll leave to your imagination.

The fact that the "club" gathered at 7 a.m., seemed way too early to have to get up on Saturday morning, but once I started I couldn't stop. There have been some extremely interesting guys who have been members of this club. As far as I know, it started with Ray Stevens and his partner, Cyrus "Buddy" Kalb.

Regular attendees were DoRight Sullivan, Don Light (always had a sport coat on with a toothbrush sticking out of one of the pockets), George "Goober" Lindsey from the Andy Griffith Show, Norro Wilson, Bill Hudson, Don Cusic, Ralph Emery of Nashville Now fame, Larry Black from Country Diner, Ronnie Robbins (Marty's son), Blake Chancey (Ron's son), Don Jennings (Bob's son), Ham Wallace (Ham's son), Jim Stephany (no one will admit parenthood), and me. Occasionally, Kyle Lehning and Paul Leim make an appearance. Do you wonder what this group talks about at breakfast? Psssst, nobody cares!

Just outside LePeep Cafe in 2017. At that point, these are the few who had survived eating at LePeep.

(L to R: Ralph Emery, Don Cusic, Larry Black, Ray Stevens, Jim Stephany, Buddy Kalb, Norro Wilson. Bending from left Don Jennings and Bergen White)

6

My Family

Before I go on recounting my career, I want to tell you about my family. Many times I've been asked what I am the most proud of — working with Elvis, Garth, Kenny, Tammy, Dolly? Without hesitation I would say I am the most proud of my five sons. Yep! There are five of them. Count em 5 sons! Nick, my oldest, was born in 1963, Marc in 1965, Mitch in 1967, Casey in 1970, and Chance in 1979.

They are all more adult than I am, and I seek advice from them every day. And from them I've gotten three beautiful daughters-in-law: Traci, Amanda, and Jessica, and eight marvelous grandchildren: Josh, Nicole, Gracie, Jack, Jeff, Virginia, MacKensie, and Bergen, (named after guess who), and one great-granddaughter, Sonja. I can't figure out why I've been blessed so much, but I must've been doing something at least partially right! God has been exceptionally good to me!

Nicholas Charles White
b. Jan. 25, 1963

Marc Kavanaugh White
b. Feb. 24, 1965

Mitchell Bergen White
b. Sept. 19, 1967

My Family

Casey Christopher Bergen White
b. July 27, 1970

Chancey Bergen White
b. May 5, 1979

The Producers

7

Bill Justis

Bill with his cigerillo. At Tuneville Recording's studio called "Back ere" recording background vocals for Ronny and the Daytonas.

Bill Justis became my employer, my mentor, and my dear friend. To try to explain how much I learned from working with Bill would be a book all by itself. He advised me once that "less is more", trying to get me to realize that I didn't need to try to show off all I know on every arrangement. An arrangement needs to have some spaces to "breath" as he put it. He also told me that ideally, a perfect string section should have twice as many violins as violas, twice as many violas as cellos, and twice as many cellos as string basses. The perfect section is what I was able to have with George Strait; sixteen violins, eight violas, four cellos, and two string bass. Perfect!

Even the hilarious little notations he would include on his arrangements, like each page of his score for a song would have a different title, each one funnier than the last one. I've done the same thing for so long that people think I'm the originator of the idea, but not a chance; it was Bill. Bill had a big hit of his own called "Raunchy" with Bill playing the tenor sax in the late '50s or early '60s.

Bill lost his hair early, and for an "extravaganza show" with a bunch of other artists he wore a cool wig to cover his bald head. The temperature on stage was a hundred degrees, and the sweat between Bill's bald head and the wig became uncontainable and started leaking down his cheeks, to the delight of the crowd. Bill made the most of it when he jerked off the wig and threw it into the crowd.

Bill came to my rescue so many times, but the time I remember most was when I was working jingles. I had been working with a producer from New York named Arnold Brown from the Dancer, Fitzgerald and Sample Company. Arnold had come to Nashville on multiple occasions and hired me each time he came. On this particular occasion though, he wanted me to come to New York to do several spots for Life Savers and Toyota. Arnold assumed I could do "click tracks" but in fact, I had never done one before and had no idea we were doing it this time. (Side note — click tracks is a method of mathematically writing music to fit jingles and films.) As a simple example, let's say a light bulb comes on at exactly 198 frames into the film and you want an orchestra bell to hit at that exact point. Click tracks can make that happen IF you know how to do them. I was erroneously thinking this gig would be a breeze, so I took my eight-year-old son, Mitch, to New York with me.

We're picked up by a limo when we arrive and are taken directly to the Dancer, Fitzgerald and Sample offices on Madison Avenue. Arnold greets us, then takes us directly to the film room. The film starts, Mitch and I are watching it, but in the back of my mind I'm beginning to wonder why we are watching this film. About that time Arnold stops the film and asks me why I'm not taking down a bar count. I'm thinking, "What the fuck have I gotten myself into, and more specifically, what the fuck is a bar count?" In full panic/survivor mode, I jump up and tell Arnold that I had forgotten to a make a very important phone call before I left Nashville. He's okay with that and we take a thirty-minute break. I immediately call Bill, praying he will answer. Thank God he did and can tell from my voice that I am in serious trouble. He says, "Hey, man, you need to take a few deep breaths and relax, man." He then tells me I need to put Arnold on the defensive by telling him, "This is the first time anyone ever asked me for a bar count, they've always been provided for me."

This strategy worked, so Arnold told me to give them a few hours and they would give me the bar counts.

That particular crisis was averted, but what then do I do with these "bar counts"? In the meantime they were having some difficulty getting the bar counts to me so I took Mitch to see the New York Knicks play the Cleveland Cavaliers at Madison Square Garden hoping it might relax me a little. You see, I still had to write these spots in the middle of the night with Bill on long distance, guiding me through this "click track" shit. Long distance must've cost me $1,000 for that one night.

Believe it or not, the sessions went well, I left them an invoice, then Mitch and I came back home. I must've aged ten years in those three days. Thank God Mitch was with me to help keep me from going completely crazy, and thank God for Bill Justis! Arnold's assistant called me a few days later telling me Arnold was very happy with the spots and she also let me know that she caught a mistake I had made on the invoice. You see, what arrangers are paid in Nashville isn't nearly as much as what they are paid in The Big Apple, so she assumed that my rate was for each spot! How about that? I got paid double for something I had no idea what I was doing. Sometimes it's better to be lucky than good. I tried to give the extra money to Bill, but he wouldn't accept it.

In the mid '60s, when the Beach Boys and Jan and Dean were so big, Justis produced a record for Bucky Wilkin, Marijohn Wilkin's son, who was a great writer and guitarist. The record was "Little GTO" and the group was called Ronny & the Daytonas. Bucky was Ronnie, and Buzz Cason, Bobby Russell and I were the Daytonas. The record was a smash hit, so we took to the road doing shows with the Beach Boys, Jan and Dean, the Knickerbockers, etc. We were easily the worst band in the show.

In late 1966, Bill took us to Munich, Germany, to do a follow-up album and a song called "Sandy". We went to Germany because Bill could use bigger string sections that cost about half of what it did in the States. I believe that album had some of the finest string writing I've ever heard to this day. Bill was magic! He reminded me of Winston Churchill, except he was funnier! Amazingly, the engineer at Trixie-tone Studio, Willy Schmidt, drank as much as Bill and never seemed to get a buzz. By this time Bill would've passed out. There's something about those Germans. Hmmm.

Bill instilled in me my bourbon affinity, among other things, and is someone who could never be replaced in my life. We lost Bill way too soon, in July 1982, but he left a lot of himself with me.

8

Fred Foster

Fred was one of the very first to use me on sessions. He'd listened to Bill Justis when Bill was helping push me out into the big stream of things. Fred was also the first to sign me to a record contract. I was working with Wayne Moss on an LP, and one of the songs was a thing Wayne and I wrote together called "The Bird Song". It was a strange tune that both Wayne and I thought nobody would understand, about a guy who killed his girlfriend and he's in prison looking through the bars at a bird outside his window.

One day Fred stopped by Wayne's studio, a famous studio called Cinderella Sound in Madison, Tennessee. Wayne and I gave him a copy of "The Bird Song" kinda snickering, since we thought he'd never understand what we were talking about. We didn't hear from him for a few days so we got in touch with him. He talked about everything except our song, and we finally interrupted and asked, "But what do you think of 'The Bird Song'?" He said, "Oh yeah, you mean the tune about a guy who's in prison for killing his girlfriend?" Wayne and I figured we wrote a better

Me, Ray Stevens and Fred at the Country Music Hall of Fame when Fred's Induction was announced – 2017.

song than we thought, or Fred was really smart or we were really stupid.

Fred signed Kris Kristofferson to a recording contract in the early '70s, when everyone thought he was crazy, since even Kris admitted he couldn't sing, but Fred knew what he was doing. The first LP Fred did with Kris was called "The Silver Tongued Devil and I". Fred had so much going on at the same time that he was getting frustrated. He'd cut all the tunes four different times in different studios with different musicians just trying to find the magic. Finally, he brought the four tapes to me with all the songs on each tape and said to me, "I'm way to close to this stuff. I can no longer tell the difference even though I know there is one. I need for you to go through all this stuff, pick the best performance, add strings, horns, voices, whatever it needs, because I'm done with this." So I did. We went in and overdubbed all the strings, voices, horns, etc. Fred mixed it and it was released.

It instantly became a gold record, and about a year later I was in Fred's lavish office, big as a gymnasium, called Monument Records. Whilst I was waiting for Fred, I noticed all these gold records decorating the walls and there it was: "The Silver Tongued Devil and I" presented to Fred Foster, and I'm thinking, "Where's MY damnass gold record?" I said nothing but went straight to the record shop, bought a copy of it, and stopped by a hardware store for a can of gold spray paint, sprayed my record, mounted it on my office wall, and said, "THERE'S my damnass gold record!"

Maybe six months passed when Fred came by my office for something, and I'd totally forgotten about my gold record on the wall. Fred walked in, looked at it, and never said a word about it. At first I was pissed, then just puzzled. Some things are not meant to be understood; this was one of those things. A friend of mine told me once that I knew a lot of shit but didn't understand any of it. Oh well.

I can't talk about Fred without telling this story. Fred had produced all of Roy Orbison's big records: "Pretty Woman", "Crying", "Running Scared", "It's Over". Jump with me now to the early '90s, when Ricky Van Shelton was recording "Pretty Woman" with Steve Buckingham producing. Steve called Fred for advice about the production and asked who was playing that famous lick. Fred told him it was Billy Sanford, Jerry Kennedy, and Wayne Moss, but also said Boots Randolph was playing the lick on the baritone sax. Steve replied, "Oh no, no, no, there is no sax on that." Fred said, "Okay, if you say so." Sometimes no matter how you try you just can't help some people.

I worked with Fred throughout my entire career, the last time in 2014 on the Willie Nelson tribute album to Ray Price. Fred was so instrumental in the careers of artists like Roy and Kris, but also Dolly Parton, Larry Gatlin, Tony Joe White, Willie Nelson.... In spite of all the awards Fred was given, I would still have to say that in his later years he was one of the most underappreciated Supermen of the music business, without question.

9

Bill Beasley

In the early '60s, Bill Beasley owned a record company called Tennessee Music Corp. He and his partner, Alan Bubis, were producing sound-a-likes, copies of "hit" records with Bill Justis doing the arranging. Bobby Russell was singing almost all the male lead vocals and could sound like anyone from Frank Sinatra to Joe Cocker. Connie Landers and Ricky Page were doing most of the female leads.

In early 1964 the Beatles had just exploded onto the music scene and Bill Beasley needed someone to sing the harmony parts on the copies of their hits, so Bobby called me. The first one I did was "Please Please Me". And then, as I mentioned earlier, Bill Beasley noticed I was extremely interested in the arranging part of it so he asked me if I wanted to give it a shot with "Yesterday" with a string quartet and acoustic guitar. My arranging career had begun.

Bill Beasley paid me to have the most fun I'd ever had in my life. Every day, every session, I was learning something as I copied hit records. What an education! I can say without fear of contradiction that I might be the only person alive who got that unique opportunity. Seriously! With Bill Beasley paying me, Bill Justis mentoring me, and Bobby singing with me, how could I miss! I suppose I could've, but I didn't. Thanks, Bill and Bill and Bobby!

10

Ron Chancey

Ron Chancey on his boat.

Ron needed an arranger in the early '70s for a session on an artist named Duane Dee. It was to be a full session—rhythm, strings, and background voices—all at once. That kind of session was fairly common in those days. (These days everything is usually done separately. Cut a rhythm track first, sometimes one musician at a time from their own home studio, then add this, add that.)

A mutual friend of ours named Don Gant was an excellent producer himself as well as great singer. He was the lead vocalist on "Morning Girl" by the Neon Philharmonic, if anyone remembers. Ron asked him for his recommendation for an arranger since Ron had never used one. Don highly recommended me, telling Ron, "You'll love this guy. You guys will get along great, and he'll do exactly what you ask him to." So he introduced us and we went over all the material. In those days the goal was to cut four sides in a three-hour session. These days it would take six months to cut four sides.

There we were at Jack Clements Studio (which would later become Sound Emporium) with a full rhythm section of fine musicians, one of whom was Lloyd Green, the legendary steel player, a full string section, background singers, the whole works. We ran through the first tune and I was discussing something with Lloyd when Ron walked up and very confrontationally said, "That's not what I asked for." I said, "What's not what you asked for?" Ron pointed out this spot on the chart and said again it was not what he asked for. I, rather indignantly I suppose, said, "That's exactly what you asked for."

Well, this went on for a while, and Ron and I were nose to nose in front of the steel literally about to get in a fight when Lloyd jumped up and pushed us apart, saying "Whoa, boys, let's take a deep breath here." Thank God Lloyd stepped in. Ron would've kicked my ass without a doubt!

After the session (we actually cut four sides) Ron asked Gant, "Why in the world would you recommend that asshole? Were you trying to be funny? We almost got in a fight." Don told him to give me another chance. Thank God he did! Ron and I became dear friends, even to the point I named my youngest son Chancey.

I remember one particular project with the Oak Ridge Boys. They were doing a song that Wayne Moss had written that had some really nice chords called "If There Were Only Time for Love". For whatever reason Ron had to leave the studio early so the Oaks had to put their voices on without Ron's supervision, as they were in a hurry to head to Las Vegas for a month-long engagement at Caesar's Palace. Anyway, Duane and Joe were okay, but Richard Sterban and William Lee Golden had screwed up the same spot on each chorus.

Ron got the tapes to me to write the strings for a session on Monday morning, but here's the problem: Ron's out of town and I can't reach him; the Oaks are in Vegas and I can't reach them either. I'm trying to figure out whether to go with the Oaks or go with the rhythm tracks. Either way it's gonna sound like shit, so since I couldn't reach anyone I wrote it both ways.

When we get to the studio on Monday morning I explain to Ron what the deal is. He says the Oaks are gone for a month and he's got to mix it that afternoon. So what do we do? Ron looks at me and says, "Can you sing those parts?" I say, "Yeah, I can sing 'em, but I can't sound like Richard Sterban" (whose bass voice makes the walls shake). Les Ladd is the engineer and he says they can do some tricks that will make it work if I can just sing the right part. So I did, and before we leave the studio Ron says, "What happened here today, stays here. No one can ever know we did this." So everyone is sworn to secrecy.

About a year later, Ron is producing the Oaks on a Dr. Pepper jingle. The session goes well and we're all in the control room to listen to the playback. It sounds great, everyone is all smiles, and Ron says, "Are we all happy?" Richard Sterban says in that basement voice, "Well, I don't know what difference it makes. Bergen's gonna fix it after we leave anyway!"

Ron slid down in his chair, so did Les Ladd, and I slid right out of the control room.

Ron produced so much in '70s, '80s, and '90s, including the Oak Ridge Boys, Crash Craddock, Brenda Lee, Jerry Lee Lewis, Conway Twitty, and Loretta Lynn, to name a few. He also produced jingles for McDonald's, Dr Pepper, United Airlines, and he won Cleo Awards for his production on McDonald's jingles.

Ron produced one session on Jerry Lee Lewis that is quite memorable. It was a full session that I arranged with a rhythm section, strings and background voices. The main song we were recording was "Send Me The Pillow That You Dream On". All the musicians are gathered at the big

RCA studio and as usual, Jerry Lee is late. He and his entourage finally arrive, and he is also accompanied by his little wife who looked like she was his granddaughter, rather than his wife.

Jerry Lee made no attempt to introduce her, just led her out to a folding chair that was no more than six feet from the piano stool where Jerry Lee would sit. This poor little creature seemed to be in a trance, would only look at Jerry Lee even though there were forty or so musicians milling around trying to be friendly with her. Obviously Jerry Lee had instructed her to look only at him. The entire session went that way. We'd cut a track, then go in the control room to listen to the playback; that is, everyone but his wife who stayed seated at her chair. Without a doubt it was the most bizarre session I remember. Seemed more like an episode of the "Twilight Zone" than a recording session. If that's not weird enough, about two weeks after the session, her lifeless body was found floating in the swimming pool at their home. Yikes! Someone call Perry Mason!

One year Ron and I went to New Orleans to do some McDonald's jingles on Al Hirt and Pete Fountain. We were accompanied by Jack Smith, one of Ron's main clients from the Leo Burnette Jingle Company in Chicago. I can't remember why, but we all had dress suits on and went down on Bourbon Street the night before the sessions to relax. We wound up at O'Brien's Pub, which is famous for this potent drink called a "hurricane". Well, as you might guess, we got shit-faced, especially Ron. At one point I got up and stumbled to the men's room, and I'm standing at this long latrine that stretched all the way across this wall. I'm doing my thing and look to my right to see Ron standing about six feet from me. He looks at me, smiles, and falls straight back like a redwood through the door where the toilets are, hits his head on a toilet, then gets right back up like nothing happened.

Somehow we find our way back to the hotel, Jack and I help Ron to his room, put him in his bed, and then go to our rooms. The next morning we're all up, showered and ready to go to work, but still drunk.

So we check on Ron and he's showering, but we notice his fine Italian suit is in the trash can. We ask why, and he says because he threw up all over it and he did the normal thing a guy does when he's thrown up onto his fine Italian suit… he threw it into the trash can. I had to ask the taxi to stop on the way to the studio so I could throw up myself. Twice.

I don't remember much about the sessions except I got to meet Allen Toussaint, the owner of the studio and a marvelous artist who had so many hits in the '60s. Truthfully, I don't remember much about him either. Whew!

Ron and me in Ft. Myers, Florida having some libations.

Blake Chancey

Blake

I guess the old saying "like father like son" works here since I went from working with Ron to working with his son Blake. And like his father, Blake has become a dear friend. Also like his father, Blake knows what he wants to hear from his arranger.

We were adding strings on a Kellie Pickler recording called "I Wonder," and I was really pleased with the way it turned out. I thought Blake was too, but when I heard the record I noticed that a certain part in the second verse that I thought was really tasty was so low in the mix that it couldn't be heard so I got in touch with him and said, "Shit, Blake,

I can't even hear that lick, it's so low in the mix." He calmly said it was because he muted it. I asked incredulously, "You muted it? Why the hell didn't you just tell me you didn't like it?" He answered, "It was easier to just mute it." Smartass.

Blake was the head of A&R for Sony for a while and produced many acts, including the boy soprano Billy Gilman, who had a big hit with "One Voice" that I arranged. Blake followed that up with a Christmas CD featuring classic Christmas songs, many of which were public domain, and Blake allowed me to claim the publishing on them. Most of the time the producer pockets that money. Not this time, though, thanks to Blake!

Blake and Paul Worley won Grammys for their co-production on the Dixie Chicks. He also had much success with David Ball, Mary Chapin Carpenter, Hank Williams Jr., and Little Big Town, to name a few. He also had much success kicking my ass on the golf course, but enough about that!

12

Bob Beckham

Beckham and me in the Dominican Republic at the "Teeth of the Dog" golf course in 2010.

Bob Beckham, "Beckrod", reluctantly did some production, but he was ninety-nine percent a publisher; the absolute best publisher in the business, and without a doubt the most generous human I've ever known. He would fight for his writers like no other to get them the very best deals. He represented Kris Kristofferson (even though Kris was signed by Marijohn Wilkin to Buckhorn Pub. Co.), Larry Gatlin, Dennis Linde, Dolly Parton, Jerry Reed, Tony Joe White and many others.

Beck started as an artist and won the Arthur Godfrey's Talent Scouts, if anyone remembers that show. He signed a record deal with Owen

Bradley on Decca Records and was on the Dick Clark Show snapping his fingers, walking down the ramp, while all the teens were swooning and dancing. His hit was "Just as Much as Ever" but soon after that he decided publishing was his thing. Beck introduced me to Shelby Singleton and convinced Shelby to sign me and release my LP *For Women Only* in 1969.

The Beckhams made me part of their unbelievable family, which included his sweet wife, Shirley, and four beautiful daughters, Pam, Cindy, Debbie, and Gaybird. To say Beck was unique is a massive understatement. He even had his very own language that I call "Beckanese". Those of us close to Beck all understood what he was saying when he would say "depeef" or "defeeshening" or "defeishening". Other folks would look at each other and say, "What'd he say?" Anyway, I still speak Beckanese to this day, as do several of my sons who either heard me or Beck speak it. I know this makes no sense, but then again, why should it?

To say that Beck and I played a lot of golf is again a massive understatement. Our golfing partners often included Chet Atkins, Floyd Kramer, Ray Baker, Ron Chancey, Ronnie Gant, Don Gant, Jim Isbell, Fred Kewley, Tony Joe White, Joe Light, and then a few pros like Richard Eller and Bobby Jernigan. Beck would set up a week long golf trip to Palm Springs, or somewhere else and I would be all in, but then one of my main clients would need me for sessions and I'd have to call Beck and cancel out of the trip. Beck had enough of this shit in a hurry so he called me and said, "Son, you let me know when you can make this trip and I'll book it—but don't you cancel out on me, you little bastard!" Beck used to sarcastically call me the product of a misspent youth. Hmm, I hope it was sarcastically. At a time when I was both really busy and having domestic difficulties, I didn't respond to Beck's calls for a couple weeks. When I finally did he said, "Well, son, I'm just ass-deep in gratitude you finally found the time to return the old man's calls." "Ass-deep in gratitude." I'd never heard that one before and have not forgotten it. We must've made at least forty of those trips to places like Palm Springs, the Dominican Republic, Naples, and Michigan. Even when Beck had to have oxygen there close to the end, we still went on those trips.

Beck had two steadfast rules concerning golf: there always has to be a wager, and you've got to be drinking (whiskey). He used to say, "Son, I don't trust a man who plays this game sober." So in an effort not to disappoint Beck, we always bet and we always drank. A lot!

I'll share just this one Beck/Berg golf story. In 1992, Chet Atkins called us and said he had to do a concert in Fort Pierce, Florida, at a golf club and wanted Billy Ed Wheeler, Beck, and me to join him for the concert and of course, golf. Chet wanted Beck to sing his hit, "Just as Much as Ever", wanted Billy Ed to do a few tunes, and also wanted me to do a tune, then accompany him while he did some stuff. So we did all that, then played golf.

On one of the last days, the four of us teed off about noon and played eighteen holes. Chet and Billy Ed were done, but Beck and I continued. At that point, Beck was down I-can't-remember-how-much and we were both quite drunk and Beck said, "How much am I down to you, son?" Whatever it was, he said, "I'll play you for it, son." So we started off again, getting more drunk and more obnoxious as we went. Sometimes when I'm drunk I get into a zone and play better than usual. That's what happened that day. Each hole I'd win and Beck would say, "How much am I down to you, son? I'll play you for it." It was starting to get dark when Beck asked the question again and this time my answer was, "Beck, you're down $240,000." As usual, Beck said, "I'll play you for it, son." Thank God Beck sank a putt from off the green and we were finally even. So we quit! I love Bob Beckham and miss him terribly.

The Producers: Bob Beckham

Foreground: Bob Beckham. Background: Shel Silverstein, Chris Gantry and Kris Kristofferson. In front of Beckham's Publishing Co. Combine Music.

13

John Richbourg

*John Richbourg sitting at his mic at
WLAC Radio in the mid 60's.*

John R. was a famous DJ from WLAC radio, a fifty-thousand watt station that could be heard all over the world. His show was always at midnight and was called "Music after Hours" and he was heavy into R&B music. In the late 60's he was producing some "soul" acts in Memphis but had gotten tired of that trip, so after Fred Foster's recommendation, he hired me to arrange a session on Joe Simon. It was so cool for me to finally put a face with that famous voice I'd heard for so long.

We had all my favorites — David Briggs, Charlie McCoy, Charlie Daniels, Kenneth Buttrey, Wayne Moss, and Mac Gayden — and cut "The

The Producers: John Richbourg

Chokin' Kind" written by Harlan Howard. We added horns, and then the record was done. It became my first number one record. I'm not sure Harlan would've recognized it himself the way Joe sang it, but who cares; it was number one. Through John R's recommendation, Billy Swan then hired me to write the charts for Tony Joe White's "Polk Salad Annie", which wound up getting me in the door for Elvis' version of the song.

John R. was famous for his commercials as well. When Royal Crown Hair Dressing was the sponsor for a thirty minute segment of his show, he would say in that deep voice, "Reazal-creasol-heasaire-dreasessing". Sold like crazy after that. Try asking for it at your local pharmacy.

I worked with John R. on many acts, including Esther Phillips, Ella Washington, Clarence "Frogman" Henry, Joe Simon, and many more.

14

Jerry Kennedy

Buzz Cason, Ray Stevens, me and Jerry Kennedy having lunch at the City Café in 2019.

Jerry was not only a great producer, but also a marvelous guitarist that everyone used when he first came to town from Louisiana. Jerry was one of the three guitarists who played that marvelous lick on Roy Orbison's "Pretty Woman". The other two were Wayne Moss and Billy Sanford. Jerry seemed to always have back problems but was so much in demand he would work for producer Billy Sherrill even though he had to lay flat on his back on the studio floor while playing lead guitar. He got so busy as a producer that he stopped playing sessions except for Billy Sherrill's and a few others. I got to work with Jerry on Reba McIntyre, the Statler Brothers, Jerry Lee Lewis, Johnny Rodriguez, Johnny Duncan, Roger Miller, Loretta Lynn, and others.

On one occasion Jerry Lee Lewis was supposed to meet Jerry and me at Jerry's office at 5:30 just before a 6 p.m. session at Monument Studios so I could hear the tune we were going to record, "She Even Woke Me Up to Say Goodbye" written by Mickey Newberry. Well, as you'd guess Jerry Lee didn't show up for the meeting so Jerry Kennedy and I went on over to the studio where the musicians were warming up. I still had no idea what the song sounded like, and I had a string section sitting there with nothing to play, looking even more bored than usual.

Jerry Lee and his entourage show up at 6:45, and Jerry makes the proper introductions, then Jerry Lee sits down at the piano and says, "Let's run through this boys, so the killer can write the strings." All of a sudden I was the "killer"! No big deal though, since he called everyone "killer". The strings are just sitting there wishing they were someplace else while Jerry Lee and the band are jamming. I went out on the front steps of the studio to scribble down some string parts. I wrote a very simple chart in twenty minutes, we did one take, Jerry mixed it, it was released immediately, and was a number one record in two weeks. True story!

Another "live" session on Jerry Lee with strings and rhythm section this time including Hargus "Pig" Robbins on piano. The song was "Middle-age Crazy". Not sure why Pig was there except maybe the tune had too many chords for Jerry Lee. As Clint Eastwood would say, "a man needs to know his limitations doncha know!"

15

Billy Sherrill

Billy Sherrill knew exactly what he wanted from arrangers, even to the point of singing licks and expecting you to write them down, and he also expected to damn sure hear them on the overdubs. He used to sit in his office while the session was going on instead of in the control room where you expect the producer to be. Lou Bradley was always his engineer, and Lou would pipe the music up to Billy's office. Billy kind of reminded me of Mussolini the way he would watch over his musicians. He hired me in the early '70s to arrange the strings on George Jones' number one hit "The Grand Tour" which really bumped up my arranging credits.

He hired me on one occasion asking me to "save" this record that he had totally given up on, and he told me he'd give me his Alan Ladd ring if I could make it a hit. (Alan Ladd was a famous actor whose performance in an equally famous western called "Shane" earned him an Oscar. He and Billy became close friends and he gave this ring to Billy.) Well, the record I was trying to "save" was a bomb, so I never got my ring. Dammit!

I was having lunch one day with Billy and producer Norro Wilson at

Billy's favorite "meat and three" Hap Townes. Between bites Billy said to me straight out of the blue, "You know, I intended to hire you to do the strings on 'He Stopped Lovin' Her Today' but ... instead ... I didn't." I thought Norro was going to have a stroke from laughing so hard. I was desperately trying to think of something clever to say, but ... instead ... I didn't.

Billy told me this story about George Jones. In the late '70s or early '80s, George was the hottest thing in country music and James Taylor was the hottest thing in pop music. So the heads of each label decided they needed to record a duet with George and James. How could it possibly miss? When James was approached about the idea, he was so excited to do a duet with George Jones. When George was approached about it, he asked, "Who's James Taylor?" True story!

I also worked with Billy on Tammy Wynette, Tanya Tucker, Elvis Costello, Johnny Paycheck, Charlie Rich, and Bobby Vinton, to name a few.

16

Felton Jarvis

The only act I worked on with Felton was Elvis. Who needed anyone else? I'd done "Polk Salad Annie" with Tony Joe White, and Elvis loved it and told Felton he wanted to cut "Polk Salad Annie" and wanted to use the same guy who did Tony's and that was me. So we cut it, as well as "Bridge Over Troubled Water", "You Don't Have to Say You Love Me", "Walk a Mile in My Shoes", and a bunch of others in those first sessions.

A few days later I ran into Mary Jarvis, Felton's wife, who was also Chet's secretary, and I mentioned to her how nice it would be to get credit on an Elvis record. So many times in those days the record labels neglected to do that. Some of them still do! She said she would mention it to Felton. Next thing I knew, on the label of Elvis's new single, "You Don't Have to Say You Love Me", right below "RCA", says "Elvis Presley", and then right below "Elvis Presley" were the words "arranged and conducted by Bergen White"!

Well, all of a sudden I was Elvis' arranger. My phone was ringing off the wall. Three singles came out with me being credited until Colonel

The Producers: Felton Jarvis

Parker (Elvis' manager) saw one of these records and raised hell with RCA because no one's name was supposed to be on the record but Elvis's. But by the time he stopped it, it was okay because I was already on my way.

After I had already arranged maybe fifty charts on Elvis, I still had never met him. One day Gordon Stoker of the Jordanaires calls me to fill in for Neal Mathews on a 6 p.m. session. He then mentioned casually, "oh yea, this is for Elvis" so we need to get there early to go through all the security. So we get there about 5:30 and go in the back door of RCA Studio "B" through the control room and into the studio. The instant I walked through the door, David Briggs shouts "Hey asshole, come on over here I want you to meet Elvis". Somehow I knew I was the asshole.

So as I'm walking over to the piano, David is telling Elvis that I'm the guy who's done all the arrangements for him lately. I'm getting closer and I'm stunned at how beautiful this man is (Elvis, not David), but enough about that. Anyway, Elvis sticks out his hand to shake mine and says to me "Uh, thank you very much"! And that's all he said. I walked on over to where the background voices were and the next thing I knew, Elvis got pissed about something and walked out. We didn't record a note.

There are so many theories as to why Elvis got pissed and walked out. I've got my opinion, David Briggs has his, but no one really knows. My opinion is: Elvis wanted to play his upcoming single for all of us to hear and when he tried to play it on the turntable, it would not work. So he called for Al Pachuci, the engineer, to get it to work and he could not. So here we are in the famous RCA Studio "B" and cannot get a fucking turntable to work. So, Elvis got pissed, threw his headphones against the wall and kicked a hole in the cabinet where the worthless turntable was. He then collected himself, walked around the studio shaking everyone's hand and walked out.

David's opinion is twofold: Elvis was trying to talk to the musicians about what he wanted, but David said the singers (there were eight of us) were making so much noise it pissed off Elvis. His other opinion was: Elvis was pissed because I was there instead of Neal Mathews.

Interviewers will continue to ask why Elvis walked out but will also ask which musicians and singers were really there since so many have claimed to be. David Briggs, Jerry Carrigan, Norbert Putnam, Chip Young and Charlie McCoy were the musicians, the singers were Gordon Stoker, me filling in for Neal Mathews, Hoyt Hawkins, Ray Walker, Millie Kirkham, Jeanine Walker, Prissy Reed and Diane Shupe. Then they will ask if Elvis really threw his headphones against the wall and kicked a hole in the cabinet where the inoperative turntable was sitting. The answers to those last two questions are yes and yes. So that's my Elvis story and I'm sticking to it.

17

Chet Atkins

Chet and George Benson at Chet's home studio recording the "Stay Tuned" CD, a George Benson/Chet Atkins Duo.

Chet started using me around 1966 and continued to use me through his last CD called "Almost Alone". It was always a puzzle to figure out if Chet liked what you did or hated it, but he kept using me, so I guess he liked it. After a performance I'd stand in the control room with him listening to a playback, watching him intently to try to see any expression that indicated whether he liked it or not. He would be drawing doodles on this pad and maybe, just maybe when the playback ended he'd say, "Yeah, that'll be okay, I guess." Wow! Thanks, Chet. I guess.

Chet and his wife Leona lived just up the street behind me on

Lynnwood Boulevard and Chet loved to walk around the block carrying a golf club to defend himself from the dogs. One day I was out working in my yard next to the road, pulling up weeds, had a big hat on to protect myself from the sun, and as I'm pulling and sweating and cursing, I see these two feet walk up and stop right in front of me. I finally look up to find Chet pointing his club at me and saying, "You need to hire somebody to do that shit! Famous musicians don't do that kind of shit." I wish I could say I stopped doing that kind of shit, but that would be a lie. I'm far too stubborn.

Without-a-doubt Chet was the most laid-back human I ever met. Whatever reaction a normal person would have to a certain event, Chet's reaction would hardly register on the "reaction meter". To get any reaction at all was a milestone. So Bob Beckham called me one night right after he'd learned that Bob Jennings, nicknamed "Stumpy" and one of Chet's dearest friends, had committed suicide. Everyone was worried about Chet maybe finding out on TV or the radio and Beck decided we should go to Chet's house, hopefully finding him at home after a night at the Opry. We arrived there about 2 a.m. to find the house pitch black. I crept around to the garage to see if his car was there and indeed it was, so we knocked lightly on the door. Zero response so we knocked again a little louder. Still nothing so we knocked louder and finally a light comes on in the hall and we can see Chet coming toward the door in his nightrobe. He peeks out and sees it's us and gives us a look like only Chet can give and says "Do you guys realize it's two fuckin' a.m., this better be good." So he led us into the den and we immediately assured him this had nothing to do with his wife Naomi, who was out of town. Obviously, Chet had not heard the news. So Beck says "Chester, there's no easy way to say this but your buddy 'Stumpy' killed himself this afternoon." We just knew this dreadful news was going to be devastating to Chet but his response was "Well… I guess I'm just gonna have to get me some younger friends."

Chet put the note you see at the end of this chapter in my mailbox with a cassette in June of 1990. The cassette had on it the rhythm tracks to his final CD called "Almost Alone". He explained to me that his original intention was for it to be a solo project but decided after he got into it to add a few people, I'm so thankful one of those people was me. Maybe I'm biased, but I think it's one of his best.

In the early '90s, Chet was asked to do a concert at a famous country club in Fort Pierce, Florida. He enlisted his dear friend Billy Edd Wheeler to join him and also wanted Bob Beckham to come along and sing his hit "Just as Much as Ever". He asked me to come as well to sing and accompany him on some tunes he was going to perform. So we had about an hour to semi-rehearse and then it was showtime.

The show went well enough until Chet asks me to accompany him on electric piano. I step up on stage feeling confident until Chet starts playing a completely different set of songs than we rehearsed. I am struggling my ass off trying to keep up, playing the wrong chords on all these jazz changes, while Chet keeps this straight face for as long as he can before he looks at me and says, "Is that the best you can do?" The crowd loved it!

One night in late 1983, Leona called and told me I needed to come up to their house. I said, "For what?" and she said, "Well, you just need to come up here." This was about a month after my wife, Carole, had died in a car crash. I thought they were feeling sympathetic and felt that I needed to get out of the house. So I called my mother to come over and sit with my youngest son, Chance, who was four at the time. When I got to Chet's home studio it was full of select musicians working on tracks for George Benson ("Give Me the Night", "Turn Your Love Around", and "On Broadway"). We wound up putting strings on the Chet and George album called "Stay Tuned".

For a while after that, people were always asking Chet his opinion of George's guitar playing. His response was, "Well, he sure plays a lot of notes." Could that mean Chet thought George's playing was a little "busy"? Hmm.

In 2000, Bob Beckham called me and said, "Son, I'm taking Chet to lunch. Why don't you join us?" So I met Beck at his office and rode over to pick up Chet in Beck's car. Beck pulled into the alley next to Ray Stevens' studios, then up behind Chet's office. He waited in the car whilst I went to fetch Chester. After we'd slowly come down the steps to the first floor and out onto the back porch, Chet pointed to a bunch of golf clubs leaning in this corner and said, "Hand me one of those." I was guessing he wanted to use it as a cane and they all look the same, so I picked one up and handed it to him. He said, "Not that one, dumbass!" Chet at his best!

Chet produced Willie Nelson, Perry Como, Waylon Jennings, Bobby Bare, George Hamilton the 4th, and George Benson, to name a few. How many producers can you think of who would've turned down producing Elvis? Chet did exactly that and gave the gig to Felton Jarvis, who produced Elvis until Elvis died in 1977.

> Friday
>
> Bergen I think you will hear where the strings are intended, I'm sure you may have a better idea, if so, proceed.
> These are not my final performances, I hope to do them much better.
>
> Chet
>
> June 1990

Chet left this note in my mailbox with a cassette in June 1990.
This was to be his last album "Almost Alone".

18

Kyle Lehning

Lisa Silver and Kyle ... At lunch after a session.

I first started working with Kyle in the mid 70's when he was working with England Dan and John Ford Coley. "I'd Really Love To See You Tonight", "Nights Are Forever Without You" and "Love Is The Answer" were three of their big hits. I didn't work on the first hit, "I'd Really Love To See You Tonight". Warren Hartman, a fine arranger and Kenny Rogers, band leader, wrote the strings so when Kyle asked me to do the next project, "Nights Are Forever Without You", I was a bit puzzled. Why would he change from Warren after such success? I was hoping he had heard some really cool stuff I had done and was asking me for that reason. When I couldn't stand it any longer I asked him why. Very matter of factly he answered, "because Warren moved to LA." I said, "oh." We've worked together ever since.

Kyle is a dedicated lover of jazz. He even has his own jazz trio called the "Leonard Small Situation". Who's Leonard Small you ask? Why would you ask a silly-ass question like that? Hell, I don't know! I thought he played third base for the Pirates. In spite of his jazz leanings, Kyle produced some of the most brilliant country records ever, in my opinion, for Randy Travis.

In 2007, Kyle was doing a Christmas CD for Randy. The tracks were already cut, and Kyle was trying to decide what to do about background vocals. He asked me if I thought the Cherry Sisters (a famous trio that worked endlessly from the early 70's to the 90's) might come back together and wanted to know if I would write the parts and sing with the gals just like we used to. Lisa Silver was here in town, but Sheri Huffman was in New York and Diane Tidwell was in LA, so it would take some doing. Thankfully they all agreed, came into town, and we finished up a marvelous Christmas CD on Randy called "Songs of the Season". Both Kyle and I savored that last opportunity to work with the Cherry Sisters. If there is anyone who loves the Cherries as much as me, it might be Kyle. Impeccable taste I'd say!

Back in the late 80's or early 90's Jeff Davis (Randy's manager) hired me to arrange all of Randy's stuff for symphonies since Randy had been asked to do a lot of those concerts. So I wrote all these charts for the orchestra that would be playing along with Randy's band. We did two consecutive nights with the Hollywood Bowl Orchestra, which was marvelous. They did a bunch of these shows, but neither Kyle nor I had ever been able to attend any of the concerts.

Finally Randy was doing one of these shows with the Nashville Symphony, and Kyle and I both were able to attend. It was a great show but neither of us could hear the orchestra at all; it was totally drowned out by the band in front of the orchestra. So Kyle got this idea that we were gonna fix that. In the meantime, Randy had a stroke, so our plan was altered a bit. Kyle flew to LA to lift Randy's original vocals from the tracks, then we brought in Randy's band and instructed them to play it exactly like they did on the road since the orchestra was written to go with that. With that done, we then hired Larry Hall to brilliantly simulate the orchestra on his synth, Kyle mixed it, and we were done.

One day Kyle was having lunch with F. Reid Shippen (a marvelous engineer and producer) and after explaining what we'd done with Randy, Kyle said, "You know, actually, this never happened." Reid said, "That's the title of the album, 'This never happened'". Perfect! So far it hasn't been released.

I guess I had a reputation with producers of always wanting the strings or horns to be louder so when Kyle would give me "roughy" mixes he would say, "You'll never hear them that loud again." And he meant it.

Kyle used to run Asylum Records and produced Alison Krause while there. When he became an independent producer, he continued working with Randy but also worked with Kenny Rogers, Ronnie Milsap, Jimmy Webb, Linda Carter, Skip Ewing, and Michael Feinstein, as well as many others.

19

Jim Ed Norman

Jim Ed with Kathie Lee Gifford and Danny Kee whilst recording Kathie Lee's Christmas CD in the late '90s.

Jim Ed is the reason so many musicians called me "Mr. Christmas" since we did so many Christmas albums together. When he was still living in LA he would come into town and meet me at the Spence Manor to go over whatever we were doing. Being an arranger himself ("Take It to the Limit", and "Desperado" with the Eagles, "Right Time of the Night" with Jennifer Warnes), he was very sensitive to the fact that in order to get the best out of musicians you need to give them some leeway. Of course, if he didn't like what you did, he'd correct it in a hurry, but in a very diplomatic manner.

We would record these CDs with full orchestra, all at once, a lot of the times with segues that would continue the music between songs so the music never stopped after the first downbeat. In the segues we'd modulate and change tempos. We did this with artists like Crystal Gayle, Kenny Rogers, the Forrester Sisters, Brenda Lee, Kathie Lee Gifford, and Clay Walker. Jim Ed finally stopped doing it that way because DJs were complaining they couldn't separate the songs they wanted to play. So play the whole thing, dumbass!

Jim Ed and I meet for lunch quarterly at the Crow's Nest in Green Hills. We discuss everything from quarter notes to sixteenths and little else unless we can think of something particular to bitch about. Neither of us can ever remember the name of the place so we'll say, "Meet you at Crotches Corner."

Jim Ed was the first producer who allowed me to be the publisher on the songs that were public domain. What a gift that was!

He has such a brilliant résumé! He started with the Eagles and actually conducted the shows they were doing with full orchestra late in 2019. He ran Warner Bros. Records for years, then retired, moved to Hawaii, unretired, and is now running Curb Records. He produced artists like Jennifer Warnes, Anne Murray, Gary Morris, Mickey Gilley, and many others.

20

Larry Butler

Fred Foster, Jerry Kennedy, Chet Atkins and Larry Butler.
An unusual time when all of them were together.

It seemed like in the '80s and '90s Larry was producing everyone: Kenny Rogers, Julie Andrews, Sammy Davis Jr., Wayne Newton, John Denver, Johnny Cash, the Chipmunks. Everything was a big deal with Larry. Many times, particularly when he was producing Johnny Cash, he'd arrive at the studio in a big black limousine.

On so many of his productions he did strings in the big studio at Sound Emporium and background voices at the same time in the smaller studio. Larry boasted he could cut an entire album in one week, including the mixing. He would start with the rhythm players on Monday through

Wednesday, then add strings and voices on Thursday, then mix Friday and Saturday and—shazam!—by Sunday you had an album! Billy Sherrill (the engineer) was always at his side for these projects.

One day Larry called and asked me to put together a trio to be the Chipmunks. I called my dear friend Buzz Cason to be Alvin, Dennis Wilson to be Simon, and that left me to be Theodore. It really made absolutely zero difference who was who since they would cut the tracks at normal speed, we'd do the voices with the track slowed down to half speed, then when the tracks were played at normal speed we sounded like chipmunks. It was that simple.

We started with the Urban Chipmunk CD, then another that I can't remember the title of, then we were asked to redo the Christmas album that had been recorded in the early '50s since they couldn't get clearance to release it again.

So Alvin, Simon, and Theodore were off to LA. This was in 1981. My youngest son, Chance, was two years old and thought the Chipmunks were the coolest thing ever. The producers had just finished a Christmas special for TV, and Buzz, Dennis, and I had done seventy-five percent of the music. My wife and I were so excited for Chance to hear what we'd done. We bought one of those brand new VHS gadgets to record it. I mean, we were super excited to see this thirty-minute special with Chance. But when the credits rolled at the end of the show, our names were nowhere to be found. The producers gave credit to their grandparents and janitors, but not the singers.

Well, I was livid with Yuletide anger. I called the producers the next day to express my dismay. They claimed it was just an error of omission, never intended but then they said they wanted us right away for another project. My response: "Well, I can't speak for Alvin or Simon, but Theodore is outta here!" No more Chipmunks for us!

21

Norbert Putnam

Norbert came to Nashville in 1964 with David Briggs, Jerry Carrigan, and Hurshel Wiginton. All four started working sessions like crazy. Norbert played bass like it was a guitar and quickly became one of the most in-demand musicians in the biz. He also quickly got into production, producing acts like Joan Baez's "The Night They Drove Ole Dixie Down", Dan Fogelberg, the Addrisi Brothers, and "Margaritaville" by Jimmy Buffet.

With Norbert producing, he and I went to London several times finishing up albums on Shirley Caesar and the last time on a Christian artist named Michael Card. This marvelous album was called "The Beginning". One of the songs we were doing was called "God Will Provide a Lamb". I didn't get this tune until the last minute and had to write the chart on the flight over with a copyist waiting in London. Michael had told Norbert he wanted just orchestra, no rhythm instruments but I was concerned that we needed some kind of pulse (if you will) so Norbert and I agreed to include a harp in the arrangement. We recorded at Abbey

Road (the famous studio where the Beatles recorded "Sgt. Peppers Lonely Hearts Club Band") with a live orchestra, not a guitar in sight but sixty to seventy wonderful musicians plus the male singers from the Ambrosian Singers. The studio looks like a gymnasium with steps going up to the control room. I was down with the musicians, and Norbert was up in the control room drinking some fine wine. I'm trying to conduct and many times during the live recording, in my headsets I would hear Norbert whisper, "Are you sure you don't want a little vino?" Never a dull moment with Norbert.

We finished recording early and were very fortunate to be able to get a hotel reservation at the Turnberry Hotel in Scotland where the British Open was being played. This was in 1986, the first year Greg Norman won the Open. We arrived in time to watch the Saturday and Sunday rounds. After the Saturday round, when I got back to the hotel, I was told I could have my own room because one of the American golfers, Craig Stadler, had trashed his room after a horrible round and even injured himself. After the room was cleaned (rebuilt) I had my own room.

After the final round on Sunday night I was in my room packing when I heard this noise that kept getting louder and louder. I should mention here that this was the same year that a lot of the American players (Curtis Strange, for instance) did not play because of bomb threats. Anyway, this sound continuing to get louder, was actually shaking the hotel, breaking windows, and such. I kneeled on the floor with my head between my legs, thinking, this is it! Come to find out after I changed my underwear, the pilot of the Concord who had come to pick up the American players was drunk and "buzzed" the building. Naturally he was fired and someone else flew them back home. Norbert and I had to get home on our own.

22

Brent Maher

I started working with Brent in the late '60s when he was a staff engineer at Fred Foster's studio down on 7th Avenue in the Lion's Club building. His first solo gig as engineer was recording Robert Knight on "Everlasting Love", written by Buzz Cason and Mac Gayden that has become a rock classic.

Soon after that, Brent's mentor, Bill Porter, persuaded him to move to Las Vegas where he recorded Ike and Tina Turner's "Proud Mary" and worked closely with Bobby Darin and many more. He went to work one morning to find that the police and fire department had completely barricaded around the studio. It had burned to the ground sometime in the night. Perfect timing since Buzz Cason had plans to build a new studio and wanted Brent to run it. So Brent moved back to Nashville, and I'm so glad he did.

Brent's daughter, Diana, was in the hospital after a serious car accident, and while Brent was visiting her he met her nurse, who was named Naomi. Naomi asked Brent to listen to a few cassettes that she had recorded with her daughter Wynonna, and just like that, the Judds were discovered. Brent and Don Potter wound up producing the Judds with phenomenal success.

Brent would go on to produce Kenny Rogers, including the Christmas classic "The Gift", and also Kenny and Wynonna's marvelous Christmas duet "Mary, Did You Know?" In addition, he produced the Dave Loggins album called "One Way Ticket to Paradise" (that I was privileged to arrange), and with Steve Gibson, he also co-produced Michael Johnson's mega hit "Bluer Than Blue".

Brent was so busy that he gave one of his production gigs to Jim McKell and me: producing the CD "Classic Love Songs" for Kenny Rogers. QVC had a contest where people all over the country would vote on their thirty favorite love songs. Kenny recorded them with Jim and I producing. Thanks so much, Brent.

23

Buddy Killen

I probably worked with Buddy Killen longer than any other producer. We did Joe Tex, Exile, T.G. Shepherd, Ronnie McDowell, and many others. Buddy had a habit of giving me cassettes with maybe ten songs on them. Charlotte Tucker, his secretary, would hand me the cassette and say Buddy wanted strings on them. I'd ask which ones, and she'd say he said put strings on all of them. Well, some of them didn't need strings, so I didn't add them. He was okay with that.

Almost always, though, by the time I'd finished my charts and we were in the studio, Buddy would've added stuff, like steel guitar or fiddle, and I'd be thinking, "Oh shit, this is gonna be a train wreck!" But somehow it always worked out. Buddy said I was like a little Volkswagen darting through traffic but always getting there. Hmm. I'd rather be a Maserati.

One day on an Exile string session, Buddy had to leave the session for some reason when we were getting ready for the second song. The strings take a break, so after they're finished with the restroom I go in, do my business, then find I am locked in the john. I'm banging on the door trying to get someone's attention when Beverly Herro, the receptionist, hears me. But she can't get the door open, and neither can anyone else, so they call a locksmith. In the meantime, the strings are rehearsing the second song, but they discover a mistake — either mine or my copyist's. For these purposes I'll blame it on the copyist. (Quick aside — a Copyist is the person who takes the arrangement I've written and creates parts for each of the instruments ... back to the story!)

So Shelly Kurland, the string contractor, comes and talks to me through the door, explaining the problem. He slides the chart under the door so I can inspect it and I fix the problem. They finish two more tunes, and when Buddy gets back and asks, "Where's Bergen?" they answer, "He's been in the john for the last two hours."

One morning I was driving into town on 16th Avenue South and this record came on that had the most beautiful string/piano intro, and I pulled over to the side of the road so I could listen more intently. It was T.G. Shepherd singing "Finally", and it got all the way into the first chorus before I realized it was my arrangement. Haha! I was so busy through those years I hardly had the time to sit back and listen to what I'd done because I was already working on something else. Those were the days, my friend!

Buddy had a not-so-secret lifelong ambition to be another Frank Sinatra so he hired David Briggs, Paul Leim, Larry Paxton, and John Willis to cut some tracks ("My Way", "Mack the Knife", "New York, New York", etc). I added strings and horns and Buddy added his voice. He was a deliriously happy man; not Sinatra, but he was oh so happy. He then took the tracks to his posh restaurant, the Stockyard, and performed them for the guests. Buddy had finally made it.

24

Don Gant

Don Gant was a great producer and singer. He was the lead vocalist on the big Neon Philharmonic hit "Morning Girl". He always knew what he wanted and had no problem telling you in no uncertain terms.

Don and I were singing for Larry Butler when Larry was producing Kenny Rogers's big record "Lucille". We were running over it with the musicians and Kenny when Larry tells us to take a break while they get the track and Kenny's vocal, since Kenny keeps changing the phrasing.

So we're out in the lounge doing what musicians and singers do when they don't have anything to do, but I must say we were doing it quite well. Finally, Larry says, "Okay, we're ready to put on the background voices." Don and I get to our mics, thinking we are just running through it again, so we're talking to each other about the phrasing, when Larry says, "Great! Next tune." We plead, "No, no, no, Larry, we can do it much better." Larry says it's good enough for an album cut and we move on. Apparently Larry knew what he was talking about. I think it sold about twenty million as a single.

Don produced many acts, but particularly Jimmy Buffett. When we were finishing up Jimmy's first hit, "Come Monday", we had already added strings and background voices, but we still had three flute parts to put on and only two tracks left. So Billy Puett put on the high flute part, which left two flute parts but only one track left. I suggested to Don that I sing the middle flute part while Billy played the low part. It worked, and no one ever knew the difference. As a matter of fact, hardly anyone would notice the flutes on it anyway. Hint: listen real closely to the chorus, "Come Monday, flute, flute, flute, Come Monday, flute, flute, flute." If you still don't hear them, you'll just have to take my word for it.

25

Ronnie Gant

Ronnie Gant might have been the most competitive human I've ever met. He hated to lose. I don't think that's such a bad thing unless you want to kill the person you just lost to. Okay, maybe that's a bit of an exaggeration. He was a marvelous natural athlete who held the record for the highest batting average in high school baseball in Nashville, with an average of .691. This was in the '50s, and I think the record held up until the mid '80s. He excelled at whatever he played; basketball, football, golf. Ronnie and his older brother Don, Weldon Myrick, Jim Owens, Pat Carter, Bob Morrison, and I used to meet on Saturday mornings at McCabe Community Center to play basketball. Ronnie and Don would invariably get into a fight, and we would have to pull them apart. Truthfully, Ronnie was better than Don at everything except music, and maybe that resentment caused many of the fights, but they were brothers, and they loved each other.

Ronnie ran Acuff Rose Publishing company for years and engineered the sessions that were recorded at Acuff Rose Studio on Franklin Road.

The Neon Philharmonic, the Newbeats, and Paul and Paula were just a few of the acts that recorded at Acuff Rose with Ronnie at the controls. After Acuff Rose, Ronnie became the director of Publishing at Hori-Pro Inc. until he retired.

Ronnie was one of the fortunate golfers that Bob Beckham included on so many of the golf trips. Naples, Florida, Boyne Mountain in upper Michigan, Hilton Head, and Myrtle Beach were included in our week long trips that saw quite a bit of money exchanged, and naturally quite a bit of booze consumed. One day I attempted a thirty-five-foot putt that went twenty feet past the hole and about fifteen feet to the left. Ronnie's comment was, "Your line was off, but your speed was bad." Read that again! "Your line was off but your speed was bad". I was laughing so hard it kept me from getting really pissed after such a shitty putt.

26

Tony Brown

I worked with Tony on Vince Gill and Wynonna, but mainly George Strait. Many times after we'd finished an album Tony would invite all the musicians to his "haunted" home on Tyne Boulevard. I call it "haunted" because the idiot couple that lived there before Tony was Tony Alamo and his preacher wife, Susan. These fools actually pastored a church that sat on the corner of 17th Avenue South and Edgehill. It was a beautiful old church with big stained glass windows and has since become Ocean Way Studios. Anyway, Susan died and had vowed she would come back from the grave. Her idiot husband believed her and kept having vigils and séances at their home on the corner of Tyne Blvd. and Lealand Lane. I'm told by credible sources that Tony Brown had an exorcism of the property before he moved in. Can you blame him? Imagine waking up in the middle of the night with a zombie-ish Susan Alamo staring at you with that gigantic bouffant hairdo. Talk about "Night of the Living Dead". Yikes!!!

Anyway, Tony would invite us all over so we could listen together and compliment each other on our marvelous work. It was therapeutic for the egos of fragile musicians. Lord have mercy, we needed that!

I always fought for years to try to get larger string sections. To me, the more, the merrier! I love symphonies, with big string sessions. One day Tony called me and said George Strait had been in LA visiting a string session and loved what they had, which was thirty string players. He asked if we could do that here. I was foaming at the mouth! Thirty players! Whoo-hoo! Tony asked how I would split that up, and I quickly said sixteen violins, eight violas, four cello, and two basses, the perfect string section, the number Bill Justis had taught me years before. Perfect! Thanks George and Tony!

James Stroud

James began in the business as an excellent drummer who brought great energy to a session, much like Larrie London. James quickly moved into production, and he and Mark Wright co-produced Clint Black's early hits, including "Killin' Time" that I sang on with Jana King. James also hired me to arrange the strings for Ryan Adams and the Cardinals when they did a CD in Nashville called "Jacksonville City Nights".

I guess my favorite project with James was when he hired me to arrange a CD for a marvelous artist from Cuba named Jon Secada, who had a number one pop hit in 1992 called "Just Another Day". The CD we did was called "Classics", with a thirty-piece string section and a collection of the finest musicians in town, including Paul Leim, Glen Worf, Shane Keister, Steve Gibson, and John Willis. It was recorded "live" and I strongly suggest you give it a listen.

After the 9/11 terrorist attacks on the Twin Towers in New York City, there was a big push to record anything that was patriotic. James was hired by the famous "All In The Family" sit-com producer, Norman

Lear, to record "America the Beautiful" for a special Lear was producing that was going to be featured in Philadelphia at the museum where the Liberty Bell is displayed. James then hired me to arrange "America the Beautiful" with as big an orchestra as I wanted, and a choir. Money was no object, just do it. So I did! Our pre-recorded track would be sung by another choir of super country stars including Garth, Vince Gill, Amy Grant, Lyle Lovett, Kenny Rogers, Randy Owen of Alabama, Toby Keith, The Oak Ridge Boys, and many more.

This was going to be an extravaganza, to the point that the original copy of the Declaration of Independence was being transported to Nashville with a six-man security team, and Norman Lear. Now get this: I can't begin to explain how this could've possibly happened, but Norman Lear owns the original Declaration of Independence! WHAT? Yeah, he owns it! So who owns the Liberty Bell? Lebron James? Being the dumbass I am, I thought "We the People" owned that shit. Sorry, but I can't quite grasp this. Lear owns it, but it is displayed at the National Archives Museum in Washington, DC. Anyway, where was I?

Oh yeah, so the country stars sang to our pre-recorded track whilst the crowd walked single file to observe the famous document. My work was done, but James asked me to be there to conduct. Truthfully, it didn't need to be conducted, but they all felt the occasion called for a conductor. So I'm standing next to a wall trying to stay out of the way, waiting to be summoned on my head set, when I hear the intro start and I think, "Shit, I need to get up there." Then I notice Stroud has decided to conduct it himself.

I think the spotlights beckoned him. Attaboy, James!

28

Mark Wright

Mark and I had a lot in common; we were both from minister families and had a similar upbringing. He was one of those guys who brought a lot of energy with him into the studio, which filtered out to the musicians, who always gave him their best. I worked with him on LeAnn Womack, Clint Black, Mark Chesnutt, Rhett Akins, Dawn Sears, and many more.

Mark had to stand with his convictions when he was producing a Dennis Linde song called "Bubba Shot the Jukebox" for artist Mark Chesnutt. Mark, the producer, wanted to add strings to the track when everyone in the biz thought he was crazy, but he knew what he wanted and stuck with it. He and I discussed it. I wrote the strings, and it was a big record!

On another session for Mark Chesnutt we were adding strings to a track called "Almost Goodbye". A couple years earlier I had conducted a session that Alan Moore had arranged on a song called "Lift Up the Suffering Symbol" for the Christian artist Michael Card. Alan had written this incredible sixteenth-note triplets up and down gliss that impressed the shit out of me, and I was just waiting for an opportunity to use it. Here it was! On the intro of "Almost Goodbye" I wrote this thing, and when the strings played it, I thought Mark, the producer, was gonna come through the control room glass window. "WHAT was that?" I figured he hated it so I sheepishly said, "Okay, I'll take it out." He said, "No you won't. I love it!"

Later that year we were doing the CMA Awards and Mark, the artist, was doing "Almost Goodbye" on the show. No big string section, just Mark's band and fiddle player playing that lick. The fiddle dude told me he was actually playing and singing at the same time, trying to capture the lick, and I must say, he did a really good job.

On another occasion my son Casey, who was maybe ten at the time, was with me in the studio when we were adding strings to a LeeAnn Womack track. The control room was full of visitors. Mark liked it that way; he had an audience, and he loved to brag on people. One of my strong suits I suppose was being able to make changes quickly, so at one point he stopped the track and asked me to change some stuff, then said to the audience in the control room, "Watch this. This guy's a genius." My son has never forgotten that!

29

Tom Collins

Tom was the trumpet playing pride of Lenoir City, Tennessee. I worked with Tom on biggies such as Ronnie Milsap, Barbara Mandrell, and Sylvia. So many hit records with Milsap: "Legend in My Time", "Smokey Mountain Rain", "Almost Like a Song", "Any Day Now", "Please Don't Tell Me How the Story Ends". Same with Mandrell: "If Loving You Is Wrong I Don't Wanna Be Right", "Sleeping Single in a Double Bed" and "Crackers".

Tom had style. He would always come to the studio wearing a white shirt and tie while most of the musicians wore overalls or Levi's. In his dreams, Tom was a conductor. Not a train, but a symphony conductor, and we used to laugh because he always rushed when he was conducting. It didn't matter since none of the musicians were paying any attention to him anyway, but it was funny. And Tom was laughing with us. If the tempo started at eighty, it would wind up at a hundred with Tom conducting. But hey, you can record more songs on the session that way. Ha-ha!

30

Ray Baker

I worked with Ray a lot, and played golf with him even more. Ray produced a lot of acts, but the main ones I worked with him on were Charlie Pride and Merle Haggard. Ray was a member of Bluegrass Country Club, and one day he invited Charlie Pride, Bob Beckham, and me to play with him. Apparently Charlie thought everyone was deaf so he talked really loud. Naturally, with Beckham playing we managed to get a pretty substantial wager going. Charlie and I were partners against Ray and Beckham, and when Ray knocked one in from the fairway for an eagle on number sixteen, Charlie could be heard screaming all the way to his home in Dallas.

After we finished and were libating in the lounge, Ray was telling us who owed who, but Charlie would have none of that. He insisted we place all the money on the table. Ray said, "Charlie, it all comes out the same way." But no, since Charlie was talking so loud, everyone in the lounge could hear him… we obliged.

Ray was producing Merle Haggard and asked me to call Merle to discuss a particular song that I was adding strings to. Merle was in California on this yacht, so Ray gave me the number and I called Merle. We never spoke a word about the arrangement because Merle had an ingrown toenail and that had his full attention; I got none. He was nice enough, but we accomplished nothing.

The only time I ever actually met Merle was when David Briggs and I were music directors for the CMA Awards and Merle and Jewel were on the show together. David and I were trying to get a grip on what they were going to do. Jewel was semi-helpful, but Merle was so ripped on weed that when he looked at you his eyes went in different directions. We accomplished nothing.

Norro Wilson

I loved Norro, just like everyone else did. I worked with him a lot from the very beginning of my career. Norro hired me to arrange a pile of Charlie Pride and Margo Smith stuff. One was a full session on a Wayland Holyfield song "Never Been So Loved in All of My Life", which was a big hit for Charlie.

In the mid '70s, Norro hired me again to do a full session on Chuck Woolery, the game show host who was actually quite a good singer. Anyway, we were at Columbia Studio B and we were running through a song called "Lonely Street", that Andy Williams had already had a big pop hit on.

On the session were two seasoned, marvelous musicians, Grady Martin and Buddy Emmons, wonderful musicians who could also be quite difficult to work with if they'd gotten up on the wrong side of the bed. On the rhythm chart I had designated where Grady should fill, where Buddy should fill, where "Pig" Robbins should fill, etc. I did that because I didn't want everyone just freewheeling it, all picking at the same time, since there were also strings and background voices. Seemed a reasonable thing to ask. I never would've guessed it was gonna piss these two guys off.

Exactly what I was trying to avoid was happening: they were picking at the same time. Both of these guys knew better, but I was being tested. After the first run-through, Norro said to me, "Sounds like a circus out there. These guys are playing all over the place." So I said to them, "Hey, guys, if you've not noticed, on the chart I've got the designated spots where I want you to fill." So we ran it again. This time Grady's guitar was resting on his lap and both of them played nothing. Nothing! Not a note. So Norro said to me, "What the fuck is going on? They're not playing at all." I explained to Norro that I had already spoken to them, so maybe he should.

He talked to them and they said they had been instructed to only play in the designated spots. So Norro asked them, "Then why the fuck aren't you playing in those designated spots?" They finally relented, and the record turned out great. After several years of working with these guys, we became very good friends.

Another time Norro and Buddy Cannon were co-producing George Jones at RCA Studios. I was hired to sing in a male quartet. It was Dennis Wilson, Russell Terrell, Louis Nunley and me. We were about an hour into the session when it was time to take a little break. After about ten minutes we all came back into the studio, except for George, who had decided to go home without telling anyone. So everyone went home.

32

Buddy Cannon

Buddy hired me in 2013 to arrange a CD on Duck Dynasty called "Duck the Halls: A Robertson Family Christmas". The project included just about the entire Robertson family. Uncle Si sang "You're a Mean One, Mr. Grinch" with full orchestra. "Duck the Halls" was full orchestra as well. Some big-name acts wanted in on the action, including Alison Krause, Luke Bryan, George Strait, and Josh Turner. It was a hoot!

In 2015, Buddy and Matt Rollins were co-producing a Willie Nelson/Cyndi Lauper duo on some classic songs. They had hired me to arrange the background vocal parts for "Let's Call the Whole Thing Off". Kira Small, Marabeth Quin, Tania Hancheroff, Mark Ivey, Shane McConnell, and me sang these cooler than cool parts that I had written. Buddy and Matt seemed to love what we'd done. Or so it appeared....

I couldn't wait for the CD to come out, and when it did, I found that the singers were not given label credit. So I called sweet Shannon, Buddy's assistant, to express my dismay. She calmly told me we didn't get credit because we weren't on the record. She told me that Buddy and

Matt had decided that since there weren't voices on any other tune on the record, they would leave them off of this one as well. What? Really? So George Martin shouldn't have put a string quartet on the Beatles recording of "Yesterday" simply because there wasn't a string quartet on anything else? Wow! Big mistake, George!

33

Owen Bradley

I never got the opportunity to arrange that much stuff for Owen, but I was able to work with him as a vocalist since I used to fill in with the Jordanaires if one of them couldn't make the gig. Owen produced Hank Williams, Brenda Lee, Ernest Tubb, Patsy Kline, Burl Ives, Red Foley, Kitty Wells, Loretta Lynn, and Conway Twitty, to name just a few biggies. He produced two of the biggest Christmas songs ever: "Rockin' Around the Christmas Tree" by Brenda Lee, and "Jingle Bell Rock" with Bobby Helms.

Owen had a unique ritual when he was working with a string section or background vocals. He would mic each player or singer separately and have them play or sing solo to get the sound he wanted. The first time I worked for Owen I was filling in with the Jordanaires on a session for Ernest Tubb and was unaware of this ritual. To my complete shock Owen asked me to sing by myself and I thought, "Oh shit," so I sang a little and he said, "Again," so I sang a little more and he said, "Again", and I thought, "Dear God, I must sound like shit." Then he moved on to

Gordon Stoker with the same routine and I felt better.

One of the few times I ever did arrange for Owen we were adding strings to some Lenny Dee tracks. Same ritual, then we cut the first tune, "Let Your Love Flow". To my delight Owen said, "Now, that's what strings are supposed to sound like!" I thought to myself, "Was it possible he was unhappy with the strings on all those hit records he'd produced before?" Hmm.

Owen and his son, Jerry, co-produced one of my last projects as an artist, a Christmas CD that wound up being called "The Bergen White Christmas Singers". When the singers were working on "Holly Jolly Christmas", Owen stopped us and instructed us to sing the "ho, ho, the mistletoe" like we meant it. We did as he instructed.

Unfortunately, about halfway through the project, after we'd starting putting the singers on the tracks—(Jana King, Lisa Cochran, Lisa Silver, Marabeth Quin, Jon Mark Ivey, Mike Eldred, Dennis Wilson, and me)—Owen passed away, so Jerry and I took a little time off, then finished it up later. It turned out great, I think Owen would have been proud.

34

Jerry Bradley

I worked with Jerry on projects with Charlie Pride, Dave and Sugar, and Floyd Kramer, to name a few, but I was most proud of the last thing I did with Jerry and his father, Owen: "The Bergen White Christmas Singers".

In 1999, Jerry called me and asked if I could meet with him and his dad about a project. I agreed, and we met in Jerry's office and immediately Jerry put on a Ray Conniff album. Anyone remember Ray Conniff? Anyway, we listened for a bit then Jerry stopped the album and said, "Can we do this kind of thing here?" I wasn't sure I understood the question, so I said, "What do you mean, can we do this here?" They wanted that kind of Ray Coniff sound on a Christmas project and were wanting to know if I thought we could do it. I said, "Well, yeah, do you want to start tomorrow?" This was gonna be a piece of cake, doncha know.

I am extremely proud of this album. Sounds a little like the Ray Coniff Singers, though. Only better!

35

Jerry Crutchfield

I met Jerry when I was in college and the glee club was doing a concert in Benton, Kentucky, where Jerry was a DJ at the radio station. He invited this trio, consisting of me, Allen Henson, and Ronnie Drake, to sing on his show. We became great friends and my first wife, Elaine and I used to go to Jerry's house and eat Mexican food with he and his lovely wife, Patsy.

Jerry produced the mega hit on Dave Loggins' "Please Come to Boston". That was a hit in spite of the fact I did not arrange it. He came to his senses, though, and hired me to arrange a brilliant album on Dave called "Apprentice". Jerry produced one hit after another on Lee Greenwood, including "I.O.U.", "Going, Going, Gone", and "Ring on Her Finger", but he and I will probably be best remembered for our work on the patriotic classic "God Bless the USA".

36

Gayle Hill

Gayle was an excellent jingle producer who used me for quite some time. She worked all over the country with most of the big jingle agencies. I can say without reservation that I made more money on a jingle I did with her on Miller Beer than anything I ever worked on. It was the first time this particular theme had been used; "If you've got the time, we've got the beer." Two guys from McCann Erickson in New York, Billy Davis and Bill Backer, wrote the jingle, and they hired Gayle, who hired me to contract the musicians and arrange the spot.

So I hire all the musicians, Gordon Stoker and the Jordanaires to sing on it, I've got my favorite piano player, David Briggs, full string section, the works. Problem is no one told me that this barroom piano player from New Orleans named Johnny McCluskey was supposed to play piano as well as sing, so Briggs is out.

McCluskey sits down and plays through it and the chords are quite different, which means my arrangement is out also, which means I've got to rearrange the jingle on the spot. I forgot to mention that after I'd hired Gordon and the Jordanaires, Gordon apparently forgot that I had been the one who'd hired him so he called me and hired me to fill in for Neal Mathews, a member of the Jordanaires, since Neal didn't want to sing on a beer jingle. I hired him, then he hired me, or, wait a minute… yeah, that's it.

So I'm playing vibes, counting it off, leaning over and singing, "Ooh, Miller Beer." We've cut it and then Billy Davis and Bill Backer ask the Jordanaires to stack our parts (that means getting paid double). Anyway, I made more money from singing on it than I did from contracting and arranging it, and I can tell you it was a pile of money. Thank you, Gayle! (I tried really hard, but I still can't stand Miller beer.)

37

F. Reid Shippen

My friend Kyle Lehning introduced me to Reid over some libations at Table 3 restaurant in maybe 2014 or so. He's a marvelous engineer and producer. He actually mixes projects for the London Symphony Orchestra. Yeah, that's right! I worked with Reid on a number of projects he was both engineering and producing, most notably a killer group of live musicians called "Here Come the Mummies". I wrote horns and strings for a few of their tunes.

Most recently, though, Reid hired me to add horns to his production on a CD for Gloria Gaynor (yeah, the "I Will Survive" artist from the disco '70s) called "Awakening", a Christian contemporary CD that won Reid a Grammy for his production.

Reid, Kyle, and I have libations every couple months or so to solve all the problems of the music business, and then the world. After several stiff libations the problems don't seem that insurmountable. Let's have one more, just to be sure! It's cool that I can call these guys my friends.

38

Bob Gaudio

Bob was one of the original Four Seasons and was instrumental in figuring out all those cool background parts they were doing. Back in the mid '60s, Bobby Russell and I were doing these sound-a-likes, which meant we had to try to copy the Four Seasons. It was easy for me to sing what the group was doing, but since Bobby was always the lead singer, it fell to his lot to attempt to copy Frankie Valli, who had this freaky falsetto tenor voice. What a joke! Bobby sounded like he was having a root canal. It was hilarious! For me, at least.

Fast-forward to 1996. Gaudio was producing a project on Neil Diamond and wanted me to arrange some of it. We recorded "Tennessee Moon" at Woodland Studios and all went well, then we followed it with a Neil Diamond TV special from the Ryman Auditorium. Both Gaudio and Neil were a complete pleasure to work with.

39

Walter C. Miller

Walter sitting at the director's desk for the CMA Awards in 2005.

I met Walter in 1988, when David Briggs and I became the co-music directors for the CMA Awards. Walter was director, and Bob Precht was the producer. I'm not really sure when Walter started calling me an asshole, but it started very quickly. As a matter of fact, if he hadn't called me an asshole I would've thought he was mad at me. Anytime something went awry, you'd hear, "Hey, asshole," and everyone knew he was talking to me.

We worked the CMAs until I quit in 2008, but from my association with Walter I met his son, Paul, a marvelous director on his own, and with them have been working the Memorial Day Concerts and Fourth of July concerts with the National Symphony Orchestra in Washington, DC, for the past twenty-five years.

In 2003 Brad Paisley was one of the featured artists on the 4th of July Concert. The main song he was performing was called "Little Moments" which was already a big song for him. As fate would have it, Brad could not make any of the rehearsals, so naturally Walter had me standing in for him, even at the dress rehearsal. There must've been 35,000 sitting on the grounds at the rehearsal. There I am sitting on a stool at the edge of the stage with a guitar in my hands (as if I could play it). Anyway, I sang it with the orchestra accompanying me and then headed back to the Washington Court Hotel where all of us stayed. I stepped on the elevator and there was Joe Montegna, who was co-hosting the show with Gary Sinise. He complimented me on my performance saying that it was a very difficult task to do what I had done and if the audience had closed their eyes they would've thought it was Brad.

In 2007 "Big and Rich" recorded a song about a battle in the Vietnam War called the "8th of November". It was brilliantly produced by Paul Worley and was perfect for a big orchestral arrangement. Well let me tell you I gave it my very best shot. This chart used the entire orchestra, choir and six percussionists. This thing was meant for movies I tell ya.

So we're at the dress rehearsal and I'm listening from the engineers booth in the middle of the Capital lawn. I should've expected what was coming ... Big and Rich's band was center stage in front of the orchestra. All that marvelous shit I had written could not be heard. Not a peep. Well, I was ever so dismayed and the engineer told me that I needed to be in the main sound truck with Ed Greene, the guy who controlled the sound going to television. So I went to the truck and Ed welcomed me to be in the truck with him to cue him at all these spots that I felt were so essential. So I'm cueing like a mad man but not hearing a damn thing. Being in the truck accomplished nothing.

I left the truck a very angry man, went straight back to the Hotel where I was supposed to meet Gerry Hood, the stage manager but he couldn't get there until the show was over so I got shit-faced drunk without him. After Gerry did arrive we continued to drink and Walter sneaked up behind me and said, "Hey asshole, there's a rumor circulating that you aren't happy with the mix" and laughed his ass off.

Walter is one of those people who made such an impression on you it's hard to remember when he wasn't there. From 1988 until he passed away in 2021, Walter was an enormous presence in my life and career.

40

The Kennedy Center Honors the Arts

From my association with Walter C. Miller and Chet Atkins I was hired twice to bring a band and singers to DC to do the Kennedy Center Honors the Arts shows. The first year was 1996, honoring Roy Acuff, then also a couple years later when they honored Johnny Cash. My band was a who's who of musicians and singers, the very best; David Briggs, Larry Paxton, Larrie Londin, Brent Rowan, Sonny Garrish, John Willis, Jana King, Lisa Silver and Dennis Wilson.

Each year after the show there was a gala banquet held in this gigantic hall about the size of a football field, and it was always absolutely packed. It was so full it was almost impossible to move around. I was really glad I brought some petroleum jelly with me. Cough, cough.

Anyway, I squirmed and squeezed myself to the bar to get a libation and ran into the show's producer, Don Mischer. He was the consummate host and asked me to follow him to meet some guests. We arrived at this round table and he introduced me to Walter Cronkite first, then Jack and Felicia Lemon, then Sir Anthony Hopkins. I had just a few days earlier seen "The Silence of the Lambs", and when *Hannibal Lector* reached out to shake my hand I almost soiled my pantaloons. As a matter of fact, I think I did! Anyway, those shows were the place to be if you wanted to see the stars. I mean, the other ones besides me!

41

Word/Myrrh Records

I worked on a lot of projects for Word or Myrrh Records over the years including Amy Grant, the Imperials and Glen Campbell all of whom have their own chapters in this book. Other acts included Shirley Caesar, The Pat Terry Group, Honeytree and Mike Douglas. For those of you who are not familiar with Mike Douglas, in the 50's through the 70's he was the daytime version of Johnny Carson. Like Carson he had everyone who was anyone on his show. I was hired to arrange an album on Mike and was invited to his home which was located in one of the more celebrity infested neighborhoods of Beverly Hills. After dinner I was given a tour of his home and was led into this big room with a king size bed, then was told that the infamous "horse head" scene from the original Godfather was filmed in that very room. Eek!

On one project I produced Tom Netherton, the tall, teethy guy who appeared weekly on the Lawrence Welk Show. He was a trained singer with the "boy next door" good looks that all the little middle aged to older ladies loved. Anyway, I tried in vain to get him to loosen up a bit since all his vocals were so stiff and unnatural. So I finally got fed up and was bitching to my engineer, Todd Cerney about how his stiff vocals sucked and I had no idea he had slipped into the control room unnoticed and heard everything I said. I spent the rest of the week trying to persuade him that I was just frustrated and when I said he sucked, I really meant he was sounding really good. Oh well, we made up at least a little bit.

One story he told about Lawrence Welk was quite entertaining. If by some chance you actually watched the show, it always ended with Lawrence dancing with one of the ladies from the audience while others from the audience joined in. It became quite the joke that when they were dancing, people would be making faces because they all smelled something. You see, Lawrence had a flatulence problem and was farting. One fart after another. Only the cast knew who the real culprit was.

One of the A&R guys from Word was Ashley "Buddy" Huey who hired me to arrange many projects. One such project was for a former Miss America, Anita Bryant. She was this beautiful, wholesome creature who became the "face" of orange juice commercials and could also sing quite well. So we're off to London to record this album. As was the case quite often, I had to finish writing this stuff on the flight over and was completely exhausted when the sessions started. I'm sitting in my conductor's chair at RCA/London in front of a 60 piece orchestra and rhythm section, with big sunglasses on trying to disguise my bloodshot eyes, when I fell asleep exactly when the contractor was asking me a question. Buddy Huey told me later that the contractor, Raymond Moseley who had a heavy British accent, said to the orchestra "It seems our bloody conductor has nodded off."

Another story concerning Buddy Huey. He had hired me to arrange an Easter Cantata called "Breakfast in Galilee" written by Sonny Salisbury. It was a beautifully written work containing maybe 15 songs that told the story. We cut the tracks with Brown Bannister engineering, added the voices that included the Cherry Sisters, myself and several other guys. As I often did, I added a few little piano licks in a few spots, we mixed it and

The Producers: Word/Myrrh Records

that was it. When I was filling out the credits I listed everyone but also added myself to Shane Keister and Tony Migliore's names as the piano players. I had done this before and never thought a thing about it since I really did add some piano.

A few weeks later Buddy Huey and his lovely wife Dixie were throwing a big party celebrating the release of this Easter Cantata at their home in Waco, Texas. The owner of Word Records, Gerald McCracken was in attendance as well as the Chancellor of Baylor University. The party was catered and we all ate outside and then Buddy leads us all inside for a special surprise. He leads us into this big room with a sunken floor in the middle and a grand piano sitting in the center. He makes a few announcements then says we have a special guest who is going the play and sing some of the tracks from "Breakfast in Galilee". Everyone, including me is wondering who this special guest is when Buddy introduces me and invites me down to the piano. I almost had a stroke! WAIT! WHAT? I actually walked down, sat at the piano, put my fingers on the keyboard, then turn to the audience eagerly awaiting my performance, and I said "you know what makes this so very special is … I can't play the piano." Thank God they laughed, maybe because they felt sorry for me but they should've felt sorry for Buddy Huey because I gave him some serious shit afterward. BTW, I stopped putting my name on the credits after that.

Artists & Writers

42

Bobby Russell

I met Bobby in eighth grade when my family moved to Nashville. We were students at Woodmont Elementary School, then we both went to Hillsboro High, then Belmont College. We always sang together; he would sing the lead, and I would sing the harmony. While we were still in high school, Bobby actually had a semi-hit record with a group called Bobby Russell and the Impalas on a tune called "The Raven". You know, "Once upon a midnight dreary …"

Bobby continued in the music business and wrote several big hits: "Honey" by Bobby Goldsboro, which went number one, "Little Green Apples" by O.C. Smith, and "Sure Gonna Miss Her" by Gary Lewis and the Playboys.

Here's a little trivia on "Honey": Bobby was so excited when he'd finished writing it, and he wanted to come over and play it for me. So he came over to my duplex with his guitar, sat down on the couch and said, "Ok man, I want the truth! Don't give me any bullshit. If you don't like it, just say so. I want the fuckin' truth, OK?" I said ok, but then he starts again with this wanting the truth shit and I said, "OK Bobby, I'll tell you the truth. Just play the damn thing." So he starts, "See the tree how big it's grown, but friend it hasn't been so long, it was just a twig." I sat silently and glumly all the way through and when he finished he says, "So what do you think? I want the truth!" Well, I told him the truth and the truth was, it was the most dismal thing I'd ever heard. I said, "I feel like I've been to a damn funeral," Bobby stands up, grabs his guitar and tells me to go fuck myself, and storms out the door. So much for telling the truth!

A little more trivia on "Honey": Actually the first recording of Honey was on Bob Shane, the lead singer with the Kingston Trio. Bobby and Buzz Cason published it, Bobby produced it, I arranged it and it was released on Columbia Records. Bob Montgomery heard it and immediately cut it on Bobby Goldsboro but they had to wait two weeks to release theirs to see if Bob Shane's did any good. (If everyone named Bob bought it, it would've been a smash.) Well, Bob Shane's did nothing so Goldsboro's was released and shot immediately to #1 in the country. All this trivia makes it sound like I don't know shit about anything but even though I loved Bobby Russell, I hated that song and hated that record and I told the truth. For what it's worth, Fred Foster agreed with me.

Bobby had a moderate hit of his own called "Franklin Pike Circle Hero." "The Night the Lights Went out in Georgia" was a hit by Vicki Lawrence of *The Carol Burnette Show* fame, and Vicki was also Bobby's wife for a little while. I know no one wants to hear this, but "Mama" (one of The Carol Burnette Show's famous characters) had the foulest mouth I'd ever heard on a female.

During my second year teaching after college, Bobby called wanting to know if I was interested in singing on some stuff to make a little extra loot. At that time Bobby was singing with a company that copied hit records. Bobby could sound like anyone, from Sinatra to Joe Cocker, but he was not very adept at singing harmony, so I was hired to do the harmony parts. The first one I sang on was "Please Please Me" by the Beatles.

Bobby and I continued with the sound-a-likes sessions, and Tom Sparkman, one of the engineers at Columbia Studios, called us the "Gold Dust Twins" since Bobby's hair was bright red and I had dyed my hair golden blonde. I'll always remember the many times Bobby and I would listen to the 45 rpm "Hits" that we were going to copy, then head to the studio for the sessions. Everything was going so fast in those days and I was learning so much "copying" these hit records.

If I had to pick the one person most responsible for my being in the music business, it would be Bobby Russell. We lost Bobby way too soon in 1992.

43

Elvis Presley

As I mentioned earlier, David Briggs once shouted, "Hey, asshole, come on over. I want you to meet Elvis." So I walked about fifteen steps across the floor at RCA Studio B to where David was sitting at the piano and Elvis stood right beside him. As I'm walking over, David is telling Elvis, "This is the asshole who's been doing all your arrangements." Elvis looks at me, reaches out his hand to shake mine, and says, "Uh, thank you very much." The introduction lasted all of ten seconds. Thirty minutes later he and his entourage were gone.

The only reason I was there in the first place was because Gordon Stoker had been unable to contact Neal Mathews, so he'd called me to fill in with the Jordanaires. Talk about being in the "right place at the right time!" In spite of the mere thirty minutes I spent in his presence, Elvis had the most gigantic impact on my career of anyone. Three consecutive singles, "You Don't Have to Say You Love Me", "Next Step Is Love", and "I've Lost You" with my name right under his on the 45s changed me from being just another arranger to being his arranger. Gigantic!

44

George Jones

In the early '70s, Billy Sherrill took a chance and hired me to arrange the strings on George's recording of "The Grand Tour" written by Norro Wilson. It was a #1 hit record and really boosted my growing arranging credentials. To have my name linked with Billy Sherrill and George Jones was extremely cool, doncha know! I got to work on a live George Jones session when I had just gotten into the business. Gordon Stoker hired me to fill in for Hoyt Hawkins and sing with the Jordanaires on "The Race Is On".

On one session in the late '80s or early '90s, I was singing with Hurshel Wiginton, Wendy Suits, and Diane Tidwell on "Who's Gonna Fill Their Shoes". After the session, George asked the background group if we would accompany him on his tour bus to Nacogdoches, Texas, for the opening of his George Jones Amusement Park. We all eagerly agreed. Well, as it turned out George was not on our bus at all, but Johnny Paycheck was, so what else needs to be said? He was crazy as a loon, high as a kite, and drove all the rest of us on the bus crazy as well. If he sang

"Take This Job and Shove It" once, he must've sung it twenty times. The bus broke down in Memphis so we had to sit around and wait for the repair. Just another chance to hear "Take This Job and Shove It". We all seriously wanted to "shove" Johnny off the bus head first, while it was moving actually. Anyway, we all made it safely to Nacogdoches.

Despite being in the middle of the outskirts of the middle of nowhere, this place was absolutely packed. Twenty-five thousand in the crowd, at least; a little "Woodstock" it seemed. On the show were George, Willie Nelson, Ray Price, and Merle Haggard. We wound up singing background with all of them, and yes, George brought Johnny Paycheck on to sing "Take This Job and Shove It". Nacogdoches, Texas, would never be the same!

When I used to live on Otter Valley Lane, I had the distinction of living in a valley with Harlan Howard on one side and George and Tammy Wynette on the other. This was at the same time when George took his infamous trek into Green Hills on his lawn mower after a little tiff with Tammy. There was never a dull moment with George Jones.

Thank God Nancy came into the picture and changed "no show" George into a different man. A different man but with that same unmistakable voice. Nancy was with him until he passed away. George was, and is, the "standard" for male country singers!

45

Garth Brooks

Allen Reynolds called me in the fall of 1992 and hired me to arrange the "Star-Spangled Banner" for Garth to perform at the 1993 Super Bowl at the Rose Bowl in Pasadena, California, on January 31. I met with Allen and Garth to get Garth's ideas on what he wanted. To begin with, Garth wanted me to watch a movie called *Zulu* about an African tribe that was in some kind of war with the British Army. There was a little chant or something the "Zuluans" were doing in the height of battle, and Garth wanted me to take something from that. I went to Blockbuster and found *Zulu* and watched and watched until finally I asked Garth where in the movie this happens. Finally, I found the chant Garth was speaking of (I think) even though I couldn't figure out how the hell I was going to work it into the national anthem.

Next, Garth said he wanted it to be a great big choir singing a cappella, so I wrote a choir chart that Jana King and I recorded using about eight hundred tracks, but by this time, Garth had changed course again and wanted me to dig on "Elton John from Australia". After all this, we finally arrived at our direction.

So in December 1992, we pre-recorded the anthem at Javelina Recording Studios. We had about eighty musicians and a twenty-four voice choir. The chart started with the choir, and I sorta worked in the Zulu chant (I think), and from there it went to a lone snare drum that started softly and kept building as if an army were approaching. I think after about twenty-one or twenty-two snare licks Garth was supposed to start, "Oh, say can you see...." It would build from there to a gigantic ending.

So Allen, Garth, and Mark Miller mixed it, and I went to Naples to play golf with Beckham, Ray Baker, and Ronnie Gant. On about the fifth day of playing, when I returned to my room, the little green light was flashing telling me I had a message, so I called the desk. "Yes ma'am, do you have a message for White?" This little gal said in a sarcastic way, "Oh yes, Mr. White, Garth Brooks called." She thought this was a prank, but I asked, "Well, did Garth leave a number?" Again, very sarcastically she gave me the number.

So I called Garth, and he explained to me that both he and Marlee Matlin, the actress/sign-language expert, were supposed to be coming up out of a massive American flag in the middle of the field. Garth was getting concerned that with all the commotion he might lose track and come in at the wrong place, and that would be disastrous with a pre-recorded track. He said, "Hey buddy, could you possibly come to Pasadena with us and conduct me in?" I answered, "Sure, Garth, I think I can work that out." I was thrilled to death and would've gladly given up two or three of my marriages for this opportunity!

So we were at the dress rehearsal on Saturday the 30th at the Rose Bowl. Mind you, this was the same year Michael Jackson did the halftime show, so security was beyond ridiculous. The producer of the show, Don Mischer, was down on the field with Garth, me, Allen, and Mark. Garth started right off telling him that I was his arranger, and that I was a small guy who would be standing in the middle of the Dallas Cowboys so he wanted me to be up on a box or something right on the fifty-yard line so he could easily spot me when he came up out of the flag. He just kept telling the producer how important it was for me to be on the fifty-yard line. Fifty-yard line, fifty-yard line. Don Mischer finally said, "All right already, he'll be on the fifty-yard line on a box!" The rest of the rehearsal went perfectly.

So there we are on Super Bowl Sunday with 120,000 fans surrounding the field. I'm standing on my box with Dallas Cowboys on my left, Dallas Cowboys on my right, with headphones on, and I hear the producer count it off. The choir intro starts, then comes the snare drum. I'm dutifully counting these snare licks, but when I notice Garth and Marlee coming up out of the flag, he's looking toward the end zone. I'm thinking, "Oh shit, I'm over here. Why are you looking toward the end zone?" I'm seriously thinking, "Should I run to the end zone?" No, security would attack me, but what to do? So amid all the chaos and confusion, I totally lose my place, have no idea where I am, and I'm thinking, "Dear God, Garth flew me out here to do this and I am completely lost."

About that time Garth looked over and smiled and started singing, "Oh, say can you see…." He knew where he was all along and didn't need me out there at all. He brought me out there just because he felt like I deserved to be there I guess. Well, after I changed my underwear, I watched the game with Allen and Mark. We were waiting in the shuttle after the game for Garth to get on, and when he did, he stepped up, stopped, looked toward the back, pointed at me, and said, "Gotcha!"

About six months later I'd hired some background vocals for Garth, and when I get to the studio he's waiting for me and says, "Come in here. I want you to see something." He leads me to this great big panoramic photo that was taken from the blimp of him and Marlee coming up out of the flag. He picks up this gigantic magnifying glass, walks over to the photo, and searches for a moment, then points and says, "There you are!"

In 1994 Garth was doing a concert with the Hollywood Bowl Orchestra so he hired me to write the symphony charts to go with his band in the concert. He also wanted me to conduct since I had written all the charts. The normal Hollywood Bowl Orchestra conductor would have none of that, so he conducted while I listened from the engineers booth in the middle of the sold-out audience. About midway through the show Garth sits on a stool in the middle of the stage and says, "You know, when you do a special project like this there is always someone who works harder than anyone else. Stays up while everyone else is asleep making sure everything is as it should be etc. We have a person like that, his name is Bergen White," and asked me to stand. In all my years in this business, Garth is the only artist who's ever done that. This man is special.

In early 2000, I got a call from Traci Greenwood, Garth's assistant, requesting that I attend a little function at Garth and Sandy's home off of Dickerson Road. Anyone who knows anything about Nashville knows that Dickerson Road is one of the seediest areas of town. Only Garth knows the reason he would choose to build his mansion in that area, but I can guarantee it wasn't done without some thought. After several hundred wrong turns, I finally arrive at these majestic gates that led to the house. The function was not in the house, however; it was in a barn that looked like a gymnasium with paved floors that led to another room that I could best describe as being a trophy/party room. It was actually a rather small group of attendees, and I wasn't quite sure why I was one of them.

After an hour or so of partying we found out the reason we were there. Garth presented beautiful ruby rings commemorating his being named the "Artist of the Decade" to me, two marvelous singers, Robert Bailey and Vicki Hampton, several other musicians, and a few others Garth just wanted to make feel special. Garth has a way of doing that kind of thing. The rings had Garth's name on them, as well as the names of all who got the award. It was a very special evening. Only Garth!

Jana, Garth, and me at RCA Studio right after pre-recording the National Anthem for Garth, December 1992.

46

George Strait

I was privileged to work on so many of George Strait's records with Tony Brown, his producer. I briefly met George at the CMA Awards when David Briggs and I were music directors. George seemed to be nominated every year for a bunch of awards. Finally, though, when he was getting close to retiring from the road, he actually dropped by a string session. George didn't come just to meet me; he was there to meet everyone. A sincerely nice fellow he is.

A few years earlier we recorded a song called "You'll Be There". It had been nominated for "Single of the Year" at the Academy of Country Music Awards, which was being held in Las Vegas, and Tony Brown, George's producer, wanted me to be there to conduct George's performance. It had a big string section and choir, so I suppose it merited a conductor.

I fly out to Vegas, check into the Mandalay Bay, kill some time on the Strip, and try to wait patiently for our rehearsal. At the appointed time I went down to the bus port to be picked up, but no one was there. I wait anxiously for a bit, thinking maybe I'm in the wrong place, and then finally I ask a guy where I'm supposed to be picked up. He asks, "Who's the artist?" I say, "George Strait." He says, "Oh, haven't you heard? He had to cancel his performance, got sick or something." So I'm standing there with my baton in hand, with no place to stick it and no place to go, so I went back home.

47

Tammy Wynette

Tammy and her husband, George Richey, always called me "Cool Licks" since I used to have a production company called Cool Licks Incorporated.

I'm in Palm Springs again with Beckham, Richard Eller, and Jim Isbell playing golf. It's a Sunday night, and we've been there a week already when I notice I have a message on my code-a-phone. Remember those? Anyway, it's from George Richey, so I call him right away. He says, "Hey, Cool Licks, where are you?" I tell him where I am and he anxiously asks when I'm coming back home. I tell him I'll be home the next day, Monday about two in the afternoon. He explains to me that he and Tammy need for me to come directly to New York to conduct this sold-out show she's doing at the Town Hall. As soon as I arrived back in Nashville, he tells me there will be a flight that will take me to New York and then I'll be taken directly to the auditorium.

The problem was I needed to rent a tux, and since I was in California, I called my sister, Barbara, and asked her to go to Bittner's and pick up the same tux I always rented, but I told her my shirt sleeves were always way too short (you see, I wanted my shirt sleeves to show out of my tux jacket about an inch or so, so my cool cuff links could easily be seen). I told my sister to make damn sure they gave me a shirt with long enough sleeves.

When I arrive in Nashville, my sister is waiting with my tux and I'm off to New York. The limo is waiting for me at the airport and takes me straight to the Town Hall for the dress rehearsal. I get there just in time to find a sixty-piece orchestra and Tammy's band ready to rehearse. The rehearsal goes without a hitch so we all head backstage for a catered dinner.

After I eat, I'm in my dressing room, where first I put on my cool black cowboy boots and then my tux pants. I'm putting on my shirt, and when I drop my hands to my side, the shirt sleeves almost hit the floor. I'm flapping them around like a duck, thinking it's funny, so I don't get too upset.

I go out into the big room and ask this little lady who's ironing stuff for the musicians if she has some stout rubber bands. She finds some for me so I retreat back to my dressing room, place the rubber bands over each hand, pull the sleeves up to where I want them, put on my cool cuff links, then the tux jacket, and presto, I'm looking cooler than cool.

I need to mention that the first music the audience would hear was this "Stand by Your Man" fanfare that I'd written that would bring Tammy on with a bang. I would give a big downbeat, and this crash cymbal would splatter the room before the French horns and orchestra came in full blast.

So we're on stage. The show is ready to begin, I'm standing at my podium, Tammy is standing between me and the curtain, and I hear, "Ladies and gentleman, let me present the Queen of Country Music, Miss Tammy Wynette!" The curtain swings open, I give this gigantic downbeat, and my shirt-sleeves shot out of my jacket like Roman candles. The entire orchestra is in tears, but they keep playing. The French horn player busted his lip whilst I'm feverishly trying to get my sleeves back into my jacket.

After the concert was over the concertmaster approached me and said, "I've been doing these shows for forty-five years and that is the funniest thing I've ever seen." Yeah, they bring in this hayseed conductor from Nashville and this is what they get.

As the musicians were loading up to leave, I found George and Tammy to apologize, and unbelievably, neither of them even knew it happened. George said, "Great job Cool Licks!"

48

Martina McBride

I first worked with Martina in the early '90s when Paul Worley was producing her. Actually, I didn't meet Martina then, since she was on the road, but I worked with Paul, adding strings to a tune called "That's Me".

In 1993, Martina was the opening act for Garth Brooks. We were all in LA to do the Super Bowl, but Garth and Martina were performing at the Staples Center on the Saturday night before Super Bowl Sunday. Martina might not remember it, but that is when I actually met her.

I've been blessed to work with her many times ever since, most recently on her newest Christmas CD called "It's the Holiday Season". Released in 2018, it was arranged by the late Patrick Williams and was recorded in LA, but Martina asked me to arrange the background vocals. So we did the voices in Nashville at Blackbird Studios, which is owned by Martina's husband, John McBride. It's as good a Christmas CD as you will ever hear! Martina McBride at her best, and that's saying a lot considering all the big hits she's had, including "Independence Day",

"This One's for the Girls", "Blessed", "Anyway", "My Baby Loves Me", "A Broken Wing", "Concrete Angel", and "In My Daughter's Eyes", just to mention a few. Martina is the consummate performer. How does all that sound come out of such a little-bitty, beautiful person?

The beautiful Martina McBride performing at the Historic Metropolitan Opera House in Philadelphia in December 2019.

49

Martina's "Joy of Christmas" Tour

Sometime in the middle of July in 2012, Jim Medlin, Martina's piano player and band leader, called and asked me if I would be interested in doing a Christmas tour with Martina, and if so, would I hire a quartet to do it. Even though I've never been much of a roadie, I was definitely interested, so I hired three of my favorite singers—Kira Small, Marabeth Quin, and Jon Mark Ivey—to join me in the quartet. These singers can read, fake, and write their own charts if asked to; they can do the whole thing.

We started rehearsals in November, when we met Martina's marvelous band and crew, then left on Thanksgiving night at midnight for our initial concert at the Fox Theatre in Atlanta. Jim Medlin was on piano, Greg Foresman on guitar, Glen Snow on bass, and Greg Herrington on drums. The string section had Shawn Williams and Erin Slaver on violins, Emily Kohavi on viola, and Kevin Terry on cello. Later additions on strings were Cassie Shudak and Bobby Chase on violins, and Rose Rodgers on viola. All of this live music was being mixed by the incomparable John McBride,

Martina's husband, and he is absolutely the best. The mix is so good you think you're actually listening to the recording, except it's live.

Martina had at least six costume changes and looked gorgeous in all of them. It was always so cool when John and Martina would join us on the party bus after many of the shows. John always told me these juicy, trashy jokes that I never could remember, but I do remember laughing my ass off.

Kira, Marabeth, and Mark Ivey led the dancing in the aisles of the bus as it headed for the next concert. Foresman, Herrington, Snow, and Medlin played cards in the back lounge. I must say, I was exposed to liquors I never knew existed, and got drunk on them to Foresman's delight.

These tours always started in the south, then headed up north, even into Ontario the first year. Each year after that we always started at the Beau Rivage in Biloxi, then St. Charles, Louisiana, then up north again, including the Resch Center in Green Bay, the Orpheum in Minneapolis (where it's been twenty-five below zero; I've never been so cold in my life), Pittsburgh, Newark, Springfield, Milwaukee, Cleveland, Roanoke, Dallas, Houston, Louisville, the Fox Theatre (this time in St. Louis), the Westbury, New York Theatre in the round, the Chicago Theatre, the Met in Philadelphia (built in 1908, before the Titanic sank), the Midland in Kansas City, and even the Ryman in Nashville.

In 2018, we did two nights in a row with the Nashville Symphony at the Schermerhorn Symphony Center. Sold out both nights! The tour added horns for the concerts in 2019, including John Hinchey on trombone, Steve Hermann on trumpet, Jovan Quallo and Nathan McLeod on sax and flute, and it was a brand-new show featuring the songs from Martina's new Christmas album "It's the Holiday Season". What a show it was!

The show was already totally booked up into Canada and all over the north until COVID shut down all tours in 2020. Bah humbug. Hopefully we can continue soon. Working with Martina and John has been the joy in this autumn of my career.

Kira Small, Greg Foresman, Martina and me in the back lounge of the touring bus on the way to Green Bay, Wisconsin (zero fun in this bunch).

50

Randy Travis

In my humble, but accurate opinion, Randy Travis is the best country singer of them all! My first opportunity to work with Randy came when his road manager, Jeff Davis, contacted me about arranging all of Randy's hits for an orchestra to back Randy's band in his concerts. This was in the late '80s, early '90s. I wrote all these charts but never met Randy, since I was not at the concerts.

Around 1995, Randy was booked to do two consecutive nights with the Hollywood Bowl Orchestra. Jeff wanted me to be there to conduct the orchestra since I had written all the charts. This made perfect since, except the normal conductor was this "flaming" fellow who wanted desperately to conduct it himself. You can guess who wound up conducting. I was not really that surprised since I had already had the exact same experience when I was there with Garth a few years earlier.

At this point I had still never met Randy, so I was sitting with the band in the green room waiting for the first concert to begin when Lib Hatcher, Randy's manager and wife at the time, entered the room with

Randy. She brought him over and introduced us. Randy is very quiet and unassuming, and the most I got out of the meeting was, "Nice to meet ya." Then Lib said, "Great charts, don't you think, Randy?" Randy managed a, "Yeah." I don't think another word passed between Randy and me for both nights. In retrospect I'm certain Randy never intended to be rude, he just didn't have anything to say, so he didn't. I've got no problem with that.

Even though I never really got to know Randy well, that doesn't change the fact that he's the best country singer of them all. Kyle Lehning's production was perfect for Randy, and so many of the records are country classics: "On the Other Hand", "If I Didn't Have You", "Whisper My Name", "Hard Rock Bottom of My Heart", "I Told You So", "Deeper Than the Holler", "Before You Kill Us All", "Just a Matter of Time", "Three Wooden Crosses", "Forever and Ever Amen", just to mention a few. I love me some Randy Travis!

51

Glen Campbell

Me and Glen at Creative Recording in 1991 recording the "Show Me Your Way" CD.

I only got to work with Glen after he'd decided to get into the contemporary Christian market. Glen could sing absolutely anything. What a voice and what a musician! He started in LA with the Wrecking Crew, a group of famous musicians who cut hits on everyone. He also did vocals with the Beach Boys before he got his first big hit as an artist with "Gentle on My Mind". His hits include "By the Time I Get to Phoenix", "Wichita Lineman", "Galveston", "Rhinestone Cowboy", "Southern Nights" ... the list goes on and on.

Ken Harding called me to arrange and co-produce an album for Glen that wound up being called "Show Me Your Way", also the name of a duet he did with Anne Murray. The last song on the album was a Jimmy Webb epic called "The Four Horsemen". Jimmy was there when we cut the tracks. He is a brilliant, very pleasant man. You never would guess he'd penned all those marvelous hit songs.

"The Four Horsemen" is about the apocalypse and is five minutes long. There was nothing else on the album that was anything like this brilliantly written song. I had a brainstorm and suggested I put an orchestral intro in front of it, ending with a high trill that would segue into the already existing intro. Neither Ken nor Glen thought it was needed, but as I mentioned, I wasn't just the arranger, I was also a co-producer, so I decided that when we were overdubbing strings and percussion I was going to go ahead and do this intro to the intro and we could decide if we were going to use it later.

Conni Ellisor hired this great string section with Farrell Morris on percussion, so we did it. I thought it might be the greatest thing I'd not only written, but ever heard, but Ken and Glen were not impressed. So when we were mixing the album I coaxed Ken into putting it on the record. We didn't have to worry about Glen since he was in Arizona with his family.

At least a year passed, and on New Year's Day I got this phone call. "Hey, buddy, it's Glen." I said, "Glen who?" He said, "Glen Campbell." I picked myself up off the floor and tried to have a normal conversation with probably the greatest act I had ever worked with and he said, "Hey, just wanted to tell you my kids love that 'fiddle' thing you did on the front of 'The Four Horsemen'." That "fiddle" thing? I don't think any of my string section would've been pleased to be called fiddlers. Minstrels maybe, insurance salesman, anything but a fiddler. (That's not to say there's anything wrong with a fiddler.)

52

Dennis Linde

Dennis Linde was the best writer of them all. He came to Nashville from St. Louis, Missouri, where he played in a band and had been honing his writing skills before his big move to Nashville. He immediately met Bob Beckham, who took him under his wing, even to the point that Dennis married Beckham's oldest daughter, Pam.

Dennis did all of his own demos, and they quickly became the "standard" for demos. (For those who might not know what a demo is, writers will hire musicians to record demonstration versions of their new songs, hopefully showing how he or she envisions the song being recorded by the prospective artist. These demos would then be presented to the artists that you hope will record them.) He recorded them in his home studio, sometimes with Blake Chancey at the controls. He played all the instruments himself, and sang the lead and background vocals. When producers tried to record Dennis' songs on whatever artist they were producing, it became a serious puzzle trying to match the sounds Dennis got on the instruments, particularly the drums. The demo very well could've been Dennis banging on one of Pam's cooking pots with dried mustard caked on the bottom. No matter how hard musicians tried to ape Dennis' demos, they would finally just give up and get as close as they could.

So many artists had big hits with Dennis' songs: "Burning Love" with Elvis, "It Sure Is Monday" and "Bubba Shot the Jukebox" with Mark Chesnutt, "Callin' Baton Rouge" with Garth Brooks, "Goodbye Earl" with the Dixie Chicks, "Holdin' on to You" with the Oak Ridge Boys, "I'm Gonna Get You" with Eddy Raven, "John Deere Green" with Joe Diffie, "The Love She Found in Me" with Gary Morris to mention a few.

I loved Dennis's writing so much that on my first album, "For Women Only", I recorded "House on Bonnie Brae" and tried so hard to ape his demo. On my follow-up CD, "Finale", I recorded "She Won't Let You Down", "He Likes to Hurt You", and "Lookout Mountain". Dennis and his son, Will, intently studied the Civil War Battle of Lookout Mountain in Chattanooga, after which Dennis wrote this incredible song, "Lookout Mountain" depicting the horrors of that bloody battle. If you listen closely you can almost hear the cannons roaring through the fog and the cries of the wounded. (The cries you're hearing are probably me trying to sing in the same key Dennis did.)

One of the greatest honors I've ever had was when both Dennis and Harlan Howard told me they would love to co-write with me. Believe it or not, I never took either of them up on the offer simply because I could not imagine what I could bring to the table, or how I could possibly contribute anything of substance to what these brilliant writers were doing. They assured me I could, but I didn't believe them. I considered Dennis Linde to be an absolute genius, and we lost him way too soon.

53

The Oak Ridge Boys

The first time I worked with the Oaks, George Richey was producing. I can't remember the title, but it was something about a horse. After that, Ron Chancey produced all the Oaks' stuff; all the big hits.

On one occasion Ron hired me to help the Oaks on some Christmas songs for their new Christmas project. They had been on the road for a while and were not familiar with the main song we were doing, so Ron wanted me to be out in the isolation booth with the Oaks as they were singing. Like a dumbass, I agreed. Why not?

Anyway, we were out in the booth for about an hour and were finally ready to go into the control room to listen to what we had done. When I tried to walk out of the booth, I felt like I was half paralyzed and stumbled all the way into the control room. Ron looked at me, started laughing, and said, "You all right, Dink?" (That was Ron's nickname for me.) I could barely speak, and when I did, it was pure babble. Ron and the Oaks were highly amused. I was absolutely stoned to the gills and had not taken a puff. Hmm, wonder how that happened?

54

Larnelle Harris

Larnelle had the most magnificent voice of any artist I've ever worked with. Hands down. He was a classical tenor with absolutely no limits to his voice. When he sang a certain style of song he could sound like Jackie Wilson, or if that's too early for you, maybe Peabo Bryson, except better. On a funky thing like "Tell It to Jesus" he was funky; on "Cornerstone" he sounded like Pavarotti. I literally begged him to let me produce him on pop stuff, but he'd have none of it. I even said I'd give up my firstborn, but he had dedicated himself to witnessing by singing Christian music and he was gonna stick with it.

I had arranged this stuff for him with full rhythm and a big horn section for a session on a Monday morning at Ray Stevens' Sound Laboratory. So on the Sunday night before that my wife, Carole, and I went to dinner and then a movie at the old Green Hills Theatre. We saw "Shampoo" with Julie Christy. I don't remember much about the movie, but when we got to my car, we discovered it had been broken into. The radio was missing, but more importantly, the Larnelle charts were gone.

I called the police and they came to the Versailles Apartments (corner of I-440 and Hillboro Road) where we were living at the time. I explained my dilemma, even told them the charts were worth at least $10,000. One of the cops actually asked me how much it would be worth to me if they found them and returned them to me.

Well, there wasn't time for that, so I spent the entire night rewriting these charts. My copyist, Joe Layne, came to copy as I wrote. As we counted off the first tune on Monday morning, Joe was still copying. I never heard anymore from the police. I hate thieves to pieces! Hopefully, though, they might've been "re-born" when they looked at my Christian charts. Probably not. Worthless bastards.

55

Willie Nelson

L to R: Reggie Young, Willie, Marty Stuart, Me, Mark O'Connor and John Hiatt. Me standing in for Bob Dylan at the dress rehearsal for the CMA Awards around 1991.

I first worked with Willie in 1969 when Chet Atkins hired me to arrange an album on him. The title of the album and first single was "My Own Peculiar Way". Chet just gave me a cassette with ten or eleven songs and told me to do my thing. At that time I really wasn't sure what "my thing" was, but that was the beginning of me finding out.

This was to be my first time in the studio with the A-Team rhythm section; those fabled musicians who had already played on so many hits.

I was really lucky that my friends Charlie McCoy and Wayne Moss were also on the sessions, and both of them warned that these musicians were going to mess with me, initiate me, try to confuse or embarrass me. So hopefully I was prepared for whatever they were gonna do. Mind you, this was a full session with the A-Team rhythm section, fourteen strings, and the Anita Kerr Singers.

Needless to say, I was scared to death, and sure enough, on the first song when Buddy Harmon counted it off to rehearse, everyone played; but the bass player, Bob Moore, was playing a half step lower than everyone else. Had it not been for the warning I got I probably would've had a stroke, but instead I never raised my head from the score. All the way through the rundown the bass was in the wrong key. It seemed everyone was in on the gag since all the musicians kept a straight face, but when the green light came on (actually recording), it sounded just delightful. Everyone in the same key. What a concept!

Chet was his usual laidback self, and Willie was an absolute pleasure to work with. He was clean cut with a flat-top haircut and wearing a jacket with no collar like the Beatles. He told me my arranging reminded him of Ernie Freeman from LA, an arranger/piano player I had great respect for.

On one of the CMA Awards shows, Willie was doing a duet with Bob Dylan. The song was "Heartland", and naturally Dylan couldn't make the dress rehearsal, so the Director, Walter C. Miller, told me to stand in for Dylan. I rehearsed like crazy, learning all the little nuances of Dylan's performance.

So I'm standing next to Willie with an acoustic guitar, (again, as if I could play it,) with an all-star band behind us consisting of Marty Stuart, Mark O'Connor, Reggie Young, Larrie Londin, and John Hiatt, and I'm trying to sound like Dylan. Walter is rolling on the floor. Willie is laughing as well while I'm making a fool of myself. All those nuances I tried to imitate, Dylan did none of them on the show. Show business!!!

Fast-forward to the 2005 CMA Awards show from Madison Square Garden in New York City. Willie was doing a duet, this time with Paul

Simon. Willie was supposed to sing a shortened version of Paul's "Still Crazy After All These Years", and Paul was supposed to sing a shortened version of Willie's "Crazy". I was sent to Willie's dressing room to rehearse with Willie and Paul. Willie was his usual pleasant, stoned self, but Paul was a complete asshole. He kept talking and wouldn't even look at me while I was trying to explain the way we were going to do this medley. As a result, it was a complete train wreck in the rehearsal. Of course Walter Miller blamed me, once again calling me an asshole. I love Walter Miller, though, and believe it or not, that was his way of letting me know he loved me.

Just a short time later I was summoned to go out to Willie's bus to go over the song again with just Willie. I went out and found Willie's bus, knocked on the door, and when the bus door opened it looked like there was a fire inside, there was so much smoke. Only the smoke wasn't from a fire, it was reefer, grass, weed, whatever you want to call it. Willie didn't want to rehearse the duet; he wanted me to hear his latest album. After sitting on Willie's bus for an hour, I was so stoned I could barely find my way back into the Garden.

The last time I worked with Willie though was his Tribute album to Ray Price in 2014. It was the last project Fred Foster ever produced. Six of the songs were with a big orchestra, the other six were with the incredible swing band featuring Vince Gill, called the Time Jumpers. Anyway, Brittany, one of Fred's daughters was there with Fred's grandson named Reese who was maybe six at the time and was quite brilliant. Reese really wanted to see Willie's bus so finally, he was taken by his mother and Fred to see the bus. The first thing Reese said was, "What's that smell Grandpa?" Willie's sister was on the bus and after stammering for a bit she says, "Oh yeah, that's the bacon I cooked for breakfast." Reese said, "Ok", but it was obvious he wasn't buying it.

56

Ronnie Milsap

David Briggs, our wives at the time, and I used to drive to Memphis to a place called TJ's to watch Ronnie Milsap perform. He was that good! When he moved to Nashville and was signed by RCA, both Briggs and I worked his sessions with Tom Collins producing. So many hit records: "Pure Love", "Legend in My Time", "Smokey Mountain Rain", "Almost Like a Song", "Any Day Now", "Please Don't Tell Me How the Story Ends", "What a Difference You've Made in My Life", "Lost in the Fifties Tonight", and on and on. For those of you who might've been living in a cave or something, Ronnie is completely blind, but I assure you, he never let it slow him down.

I remember back in the late '70s or early '80s, Ronnie was being pressured by his label to change the musicians and arrangers he was using, to "freshen his sound", they thought. Ronnie and his partner and co-producer Rob Galbreath would not go along with the idea since they felt like they were already using the best. When Ronnie was asked to move on to another arranger, he replied, "Why would I do that? If you don't like what he's written he can change the whole arrangement in fifteen minutes."

One day Ronnie called and asked me to come over to his home on Curtiswood Lane to go over some stuff we were going to record. He met me at the back door, told me to follow him down one hall, then another, then another, and finally into his living room where the grand piano was. He sat down and played and sang, showing me the song and sort of telling me what he wanted. I took notes, and when we were done, as we were walking out, he said, "Wait a minute. I want you to see my ham radio room." Then he started walking up these stairs to the second floor and into this room where he began pointing out all these cool monitors and gadgets, then suddenly he stopped, reached over, turned on the lights, and said, "Sorry, I forget you people need light!"

57

Kenny Rogers

I was fortunate enough to work with Kenny probably longer than I have with any other artist. He was the most normal guy you could ever meet and was such a pleasure to work with. My first project with Kenny came in 1974 with Jim Ed Norman producing a Christmas record called "Christmas in America", and a song by the same title Kenny co-wrote with Dolly Parton. This was one of those Jim Ed projects where it was done with full orchestra, rhythm and background voices, all at once. It sold a million the first Christmas it was out, and I received one of the biggest checks of my life because Jim Ed allowed me to be the publisher on all the public domain songs on the album.

After Jim Ed, Larry Butler produced Kenny, then Brent Maher, then Jim McKell and I produced Kenny's "Classic Love Songs", then Kyle Lehning produced Kenny. Kenny joked at the last session we did, for "Once Again It's Christmas", that he had kept me working for fifty years. He was correct!

Back in the '80s we were cutting tracks with Brent Maher producing and Kenny said he loved my cowboy boots. He kept gawking at them until I finally said, "Do you want 'em?" He did, but they wouldn't fit, so I ordered him some boots just like mine and gave them to him the next time I saw him. He had a deluxe George Foreman grill delivered to my house to thank me.

Kenny invited me to visit his home in Athens, Georgia, and play on his private eighteen hole golf course. Yes, that's what I said, his private eighteen hole golf course. He excitedly described how he would actually cut the fairways himself when he wasn't on the road. Willie Nelson had earlier invited me to come to Texas and play on his private eighteen hole golf course. Regrettably, I never took them up on the invitation. What the hell was I thinking?

Kira Small, Kenny, Me, Mark Ivey, Lisa Silver, Shane McConnell and Tania Hancheroff at the Compound Studio after recording Kenny's "Once Upon a Christmas" album with Kyle Lehning producing.

58

Marty Robbins

In the late '50s I was a half-ass student at Hillsboro High School. A friend of the family from Woodmont Baptist Church named Frank Gonzales had given me a little part-time job assisting him with his photography. "Assisting him" meant I held the lights while he took photos. One of the gigs he did weekly was cover the stockcar races at Nashville Speedway. At that time, the most well-known drivers were Bob Reuther, Coo Coo Marlin, and Marty Robbins. I didn't meet Marty at that time though, just held the lights while his photo was taken.

I finally did meet him in the early '80s when Gordon Stoker of the Jordanaires hired me to fill in for Hoyt Hawkins on one of Marty's sessions. Gordon jokingly told me to bring my oxygen tank along since normally Marty wanted the background singers to sing all the way through. Marty was a marvelous artist but also quite the practical joker.

The session was at Columbia Studio A, and all the musicians and singers were on time and ready to go except the pianist, Bill Pursell, who bopped in about twenty minutes late. Being late was not that unusual for him, but on this occasion he had a wad of cash in his right hand that looked like he'd robbed a bank on the way over. He laid the wad on the right side of the piano so everyone could be impressed. Of course everyone noticed the wad of cash, particularly Marty.

On the first musicians break, Marty sneaks to the piano and puts Bill's wad into his pocket. Everyone is coming back into the studio, laughing at a nasty joke Marty has told, until Bill shrieks in horror that his wad is gone. After completely losing his composure, he runs out to his car, thinking maybe he left it there. Marty, with a devilish look on his face, puts the wad back on the piano. Everyone in the studio and control room is in hysterics when Bill comes back to discover his wad wasn't gone at all.

We actually did record a tune that night; "My Woman, My Woman, My Wife" was a big record for Marty.

59

Steve Wariner

Steve is almost too normal and too nice to be such a success in this business. Don't you have to screw someone over to make it? I guess not! Steve was a devoted disciple of Chet Atkins. He actually recorded an album after Chet's death that was called, "Steve Wariner C.G.P.". C.G.P. stands for "certified guitar player" which is what Chet called himself. It is completely appropriate that Steve would use that title and I'm positive Chet would be very pleased. The album is a tribute to Chet and even features a song that Steve wrote about Chet's wife Leona. It features Steve playing in Chet's "world famous" finger-picking style, and again I'm sure Chet would be pleased.

I was very pleased myself to arrange Steve's recording of "Holes in the Floor of Heaven", produced by Chet for RCA, that won Best Song at the CMA Awards that year. It was performed on the Awards Show with a string quartet consisting of Pam Sixfin, Carl Gorodetsky, Kris Wilkinson and Bob Mason, with Farrell Morris on percussion. Steve then honored me by presenting a Platinum Album to me in a ceremony at the Ryman. I guess normal and nice works sometimes!

60

Dolly Parton

I first met Dolly in the mid '60s when Bobby Russell, Dolly, and I were singing on demos. Mind you, this was "pre-boob job" Dolly, though she had a pretty nice rack already. Anyway, she was a cute little sassy talented gal, and the three of us had a really nice blend.

Fast-forward to "post-boob job" Dolly in the early '90s. Ricky Skaggs was producing Dolly on a wonderful Christian song called "He's Alive". I did the arrangements with rhythm, a big string section, and the Christ Church Choir. It was a marvelous record, and Dolly was doing it on the CMA Awards. David Briggs and I were the music directors of the show at that time, and we were pre-recording the track at Music Mill Studios on 18th Avenue South. Now, this is primo Dolly Parton: I was leaning over the console talking to the musicians when Dolly pinched me on the rear and said, "Anybody ever tell you you've got a cute ass?" Well, I began prancing around the control room feeling pretty damn good about myself until Briggs told me my ass was not that cute.

When we did the CMA Awards in New York in 2005, Dolly was doing a duet with Sir Elton John. The stage crew had constructed a circular stage about ten feet high, with just enough room on it for a bright red grand piano that Elton would be sitting at while Dolly would come up the other side. Sir Elton would start the duo singing and playing "Imagine", the John Lennon tune. About forty-five seconds into it, Dolly would come up the other side singing with Elton. Turns out, Elton could not make the dress rehearsal, so Walter Miller wanted me to sit in for Elton. Dolly knew someone was going to sit in for Elton, but she didn't know it was me. "Imagine" was so simple, even I could play it on the piano.

On the lunch break before the dress rehearsal I caught a cab to a nearby novelty shop and found the goofiest pair of sunglasses that were so big they almost covered my entire face and had a bunch of glitter on them. So I'm sitting up on the stage playing and singing, and here comes Dolly up the other side, and when she sees me she almost falls off the stage laughing. She says, "I can't sing and look at that at the same time!"

The spot went really well on the show, but Elton's sunglasses weren't nearly as cool as mine. Dolly has never changed from that cute little sassy talented gal, and she never will.

David Briggs, me and Dolly at Music Mill Recording Studio pre-recording Dolly's hit "He's Alive" for the CMA Awards in 1989.

61

Roy Orbison

Roy Orbison is one of the nicest guys I've ever met. I never worked on any of his big records, but I still have some really pleasant memories about working with him. I think it might have been in the late '70s or early '80s, but Roy's friend, and sometimes co-writer, Joe Melson was producing this one song on Roy that I was arranging for MGM Records. It was in the big studio at Woodland and must've had sixty musicians, wall-to-wall, totally live with a big string section, a full rhythm section, six background singers, and a percussionist.

Once again, I cannot remember the title of the song, but it got really big on the chorus with Roy singing at the top of his register. I'm not exaggerating when I tell you we did sixteen takes, all the way through, with Roy belting it out on each take. My vocal chords were aching just listening to Roy, but he never complained. I was the one who was complaining. My arms were getting sore from conducting. I kept glaring at Melson, trying to communicate, "What the hell are you doing?" That's just an example of what a nice guy Roy was to put up with it. Musicians have a term for when you've recorded something over and over, long since passed when it was good. The term is, "you've burned the beans". Let me tell you, these beans were scorched! Melson didn't have a clue.

Roy's performances with the Traveling Wilburys were priceless. No one but Roy sounded like Roy. I'm so glad Fred Foster saw something in the beginning that no one else was seeing. By the way, that famous guitar lick on "Pretty Woman" was Roy's idea. Wayne Moss, Jerry Kennedy and Billy Sanford played it, but it was Roy's lick.

My friend David Briggs was working a session with Roy at Eleven-Eleven Sound and left me a message to call him. When I called I heard the engineer telling David on his head set that I was on the phone. The voice that answered was Roy trying to sound like David; he just wanted to say hello. As I said, one of the nicest guys I've ever met.

I always thought John Belushi's impression of Roy on "Saturday Night Live" was one of the funniest things I ever saw on that show. Roy was an incomparable artist, for sure.

62

Lee Greenwood

I worked on a lot of Lee's stuff, with Jerry Crutchfield producing. I never got to know Lee well since he was never there when we did the string overdubs. He had so many number one hits, including "I.O.U.", "Ring on Her Finger", "Going, Going, Gone", and the massive patriotic hit "God Bless the USA".

I had taken my squeeze Mikhel to Las Vegas for a little vacation. We went to a bunch of shows, and one afternoon we went to this big shopping center right across from the Bellagio Hotel. This is the hotel with a massive pond and fountains that spray all kinds of different designs to the rhythm of music over the loud speakers. As we came out of the shopping center, the fountains were spraying to "God Bless the USA". It almost brought tears to my eyes.

If that didn't bring tears, this next story will, and I'm certain you're gonna be wondering what the hell this has to do with Lee Greenwood, but stick with me.

In a moment of sheer madness, my last wife, (I'll call her Jezebel), and I booked a Carnival Cruise from Miami, Florida to Cozumel, Mexico. Neither of us had ever been on a cruise before and were coaxed into it by her sister and brother-in-law. As fate would have it, a few months after booking the trip, we filed for divorce but decided to go anyway in another moment of sheer madness. I immediately got sea sick, but that was the least of my problems. By the way, if you've never been to Cozumel I would strongly suggest you don't, since it's one of the ugliest places I've ever seen. Why would anyone go to this place on purpose?

Very quickly "Jezebel" and I couldn't stand the sight of each other. I'd always thought a cruise would be absolutely wonderful for a couple that was madly in love. Haha, we weren't! Since there was nothing else to do that I cared anything about on this boat but have sex or get drunk, I got really drunk.

I've always hated live music, but since I was so bored I decided to go to a band concert in the theatre. About forty-five minutes into the show, the bandleader opened the stage for anyone in the audience that wanted to sing, and this "crack" band would accompany them.

So this rather portly British gentleman who thought he was Pavarotti stepped up on stage and announced he was going to sing Lee Greenwood's "God Bless the USA" in the key of D. The band sounds a chord and here he goes, "From the lakes of Minnesota, to the hills of Tennessee". It was already wrong since that's not even the lyrics to the first verse. He really wasn't that bad but the band sounded like they were playing "Jingle Bells" behind him. At first it was funny but quickly became torturous to listen to. I excused myself and went straight to the bar just outside the theatre's doors. By this time the bartender knew me well and brought me a stiff bourbon on the rocks and I asked him to give me a pen and something to write on. He obliged and I started with, "To keep you guys from butchering 'God Bless the USA' again, here are the correct chords in the key of D." I handed the bartender a $50 and asked him to place my note in the hands of the bandleader. I spent the rest of the night in the bar since I wasn't about to go to our little bitty room where "Jezebel" was. We finally docked in Cozumel where I did something else I hate… I went fishing.

There are a few notable things I learned from this ill-fated trip … cruises to Cozumel suck, as do fishing and live music, and never, ever get married again but … "GOD BLESS the USA".

63

Kathy Lee Gifford

Kathy at RCA Studio recording her Christmas CD.

Jim Ed Norman hired me to arrange both a secular and a Christmas album for Kathie Lee. She was absolutely delightful to work with. She brought the same energy to the recording studio that you saw every morning with Regis Philbin on ABC.

Both of these projects were actually double albums, so we spent a lot of time in the studio with her. She gave all the musicians (and there were a lot) a bottle of Dom Perignon at the end of each project. Walter C. Miller then hired me to be the music director on the "Kathie Lee Gifford Christmas Special" in New York City. Country star Collin Raye's segment was filmed at Wollman Rink in Central Park. The fabulous a cappella group Take 6's part was filmed at FAO Schwarz in Rockefeller Center. The gorgeous Vanessa Williams was filmed at St. Patrick's Cathedral, and the Reverend Billy Graham was filmed at Kathie Lee and Frank Gifford's home. Everything about Kathie Lee made me want to smile, and my face does not do that easily.

64

Ray Stevens

I knew Ray casually over the years, but I didn't get to know him well until I joined the "Breakfast Club" group about ten years ago. He's had so many big hit records, including "Ahab the Arab", "Gitarzan", "The Streak", "Everything Is Beautiful", "Misty", "Mr. Businessman"... the list is endless.

Back in the early '70s, Ray was being courted by one of the big TV networks to host a late night talk show, like Johnny Carson was doing. Ray might not even remember it, but he called asking if I would be interested in being his Doc Severinsen. Of course I was interested, but the show never materialized. However, the "Ray Stevens Show" is presently on several networks as I write.

One story Ray doesn't like to remember is when he was approached about doing the vocal on "Raindrops Keep Falling on My Head" for the movie "Butch Cassidy and the Sundance Kid". Ray was feverishly working on "Mr. Businessman" at the time and turned down the gig. B.J. Thomas, who had a massive hit with the song, was very appreciative.

Ray and I hardly ever worked together since he didn't need me at all. He was a marvelous arranger himself, as well as a great piano player, vocalist, comedian, and just about anything else you might think of. At the CabaRay, his marvelous Las Vegas–style showroom in Nashville, he displays all of these skills in an hour and forty-five minute show. If you've never seen Ray live, I highly recommend that you fit it into your future plans. Watching his facial contortions on "It's Me Again Margaret" and "Gitarzan" is worth the price of admission itself. He could do an entire show just focusing on any one of these aforementioned skills, but he packs them all in. If you're not completely mesmerized by his vocals and piano expertise, he'll finish you off with his laid-back skills as a comedian. The intermission is necessary to keep people from wetting their pantaloons because they don't want to miss any of the show.

I've got to say that one of my proudest moments was when Ray asked me to arrange the strings for several projects he did recently for Curb Records. I was not aware of it at the time, but John, Ray's brother, informed me that this was the first time Ray had ever hired an arranger. He always did it himself, and did it extremely well. Ray assured me that he needed my particular skills, but I still think he just didn't have the time to write thirty ballad arrangements. I had the time.

Ray was also a fine architect who wound up drawing the plans for the CabaRay. I was honored to be asked to conduct the orchestra at the opening of the CabaRay in 2019. In my life I've known very few people I would consider to be a genius. Ray Stevens is one. I'm proud to call "Raymone" a dear friend. There is absolutely no one whose talent surpasses that of Ray Stevens. No one!

Ray, Jim Stephany and me at a reception at Ray's old TV Studio.

65

Brenda Lee

Jana King and Brenda sitting in the audience watching Moody Blue rehearsal.

Before I got into the music business and was teaching at Fairview Elementary School, I'd let the students bring in their favorite records to play during our breaks. So many of them would bring in Brenda Lee 45s. "All Alone Am I", "I'm Sorry", "Sweet Nothin's", "Heart in Hand", and "Rockin' around the Christmas Tree", to name a few. This was in '63 and '64, and even though she was still a teenager, she was already a legend.

In early 1992, Brenda asked me to bring all her road charts up-to-date and if I would also sing background with her at the Montreux Jazz

Festival in Montreux, Switzerland, in July of that year. We needed another singer so Jana King joined us. My wife (for a few more months), Renee, accompanied me on the trip. One last fling I suppose.

I was in our hotel room one day when Renee called and told me I need to come down to the swimming pool immediately. I asked, "For what?" She said, "Get down here. You won't be sorry." So I went to the pool to find my wife (for a little less than a few more months) conversing with Quincy Jones and his little cutie, whose name escapes me. Renee introduced me to Quincy, who was so excited to meet me. Haha! Our lively conversation was ever so compelling and lasted about thirty seconds if I stretch it. Geez, he was so excited!

Quincy was co-producing the festival that year and the show was jam-packed with big acts. Toto, Miles Davis, Deep Purple, and The Moody Blues were all on the show, but Brenda stole it. Seriously, stole it! She was magnificent! Anyone who ever saw Brenda live will remember this, but when she was singing she could actually bend her head back so far as to almost hit her head on the stage and belt out a song at the same time. The sold-out crowd loved her!

I was fortunate enough to get to work with Brenda when both Jim Ed Norman and Ron Chancey were producing. But no matter who did the producing, Brenda was always the same. "Miss DYNAMITE!"

66

Eddy Arnold

I am quite certain that if Eddy Arnold hadn't been a very successful recording artist and TV show host, he would've been a successful politician (if there is such a thing) or (if that's not an oxymoron).

I was privileged to arrange a full session with rhythm, strings, and the Anita Kerr Singers for Eddy with Chet Atkins producing in the late '70s. The song was "Welcome to My World", which seemed to have been written for Eddy, even though it was not. Eddy was a crossover artist who had his own weekly, hour-long variety show on television. A nicer, more genuine person, you could not find. He was one of those guys who made an immediate impression on you, especially if he shook your hand.

In an unfortunate incident in the early '80s that needs not be elaborated on, I broke both of my little fingers and had them in small casts for about a month or so. After I'd decided I didn't need the casts anymore, I removed them, thinking I would just be extra careful, doncha know. So I'm working a session at RCA and we're on a little break when Eddy drops by for some reason. He's greeting everyone like a politician would, and when he gets to me he throws his left arm around my neck and grabs my right hand to shake it and I literally go to my knees in agony.

When Eddy Arnold shook your hand, you knew it had been shaken. And he got my vote.

67

The Chipmunks

From left, Simon, Alvin and Theodore. That's me pulling the strings from behind.

I've already told you about how I began with the Chipmunks, but I wanted to mention this one episode when Buzz, Dennis, and I were in LA re-recording the Chipmunks Christmas album. It had been a big hit years before when Ross Bagdasarian Sr. came up with Chipmunks idea and did the first Christmas album in the '50s. However, we were working with Ross' son, Ross Jr., and his wife, Janice Karman. I'm assuming Ross Sr. knew what he was doing, but I can tell you, Ross Jr. and his wife knew nothing. They had simply inherited this musical property but were needing to re-record the Christmas album because they couldn't get clearance to re-release the original.

We were in the midst of recording one of the tunes when Janice decided she wanted Theodore to sing the lead instead of Alvin, just for a change. Buzz, Dennis, and I knew it would make absolutely no difference and tried to explain it to them, but they insisted, so I sang the lead. About halfway through they stopped us and asked if I could sing the lead a little higher. Well, the lead is either where it is or an octave higher or an octave lower, there's no in between, but they didn't understand. If I had sung it an octave higher in falsetto even the dogs couldn't have heard it. They said, "No, no, we want it to be just a little higher than what I was singing," and I tried to explain if I sang a third higher it would be a harmony part. They said, "No, no, we still want it to be the lead." We then tried to explain to them that if they want the lead to be higher they would need to cut a new track in a higher key. Still they did not understand.

Finally, I said, as cheerfully as I could manage, "Hey, how about Simon singing it?", thinking maybe he could convince them it's higher. Still they were unhappy. The Chipmunks decided we needed a break at that point. We went out in the hall and feverishly started singing "I Saw the Light" with an old upright piano just to try to calm our nerves. The Chipmunks were highly frustrated!

68

Joe Simon

My first gold record was in 1969 with Joe Simon on the Harlan Howard tune "The Chokin' Kind". The first session I worked with THE John R. producing. It was a #1 R&B record and paved the way for "Polk Salad Annie" and all else that followed.

Joe was up for the R&B Record of the Year at the Grammys. The show was in New York City, so I took my then-wife Linda to the Big Apple for the show. It was the same year Ronnie Milsap was up for an award and Burl Ives introduced him as Ronnie Misslap. Ouch!

My only sighting of Joe Simon was when he walked down this big flight of stairs, measuring each step, in a full-length white fur coat. I mean, from his chin to his toes. If he'd thrown a few gold bobby pins, I'd have sworn it was "Gorgeous George". Almost.

69

Jimmy Buffett

In the late '60s, Jimmy Buffett wasn't "Jimmy Buffett" yet, but was a writer for *Billboard Magazine*. I was getting pretty hot as an arranger when Jimmy called and wanted to meet me at Fuddruckers for an interview. Now, how cool is that? Jimmy Buffett interviewed me instead of the other way around.

Only a few years later Don Gant called on me to arrange "Come Monday" for Buffett. It had strings naturally and was a prime example of how mixing strings in with the steel guitar can be marvelous, particularly when the steel player is Weldon Myrick. Don and I sang the background vocals and "Come Monday" was the beginning of Jimmy becoming "Jimmy".

Don, Buzz Cason, and I added backgrounds to Jimmy's next two or three albums. Jimmy was a real hoot to work with. We did some of the overdubs in Murfreesboro at Chip Young's studio called Boxwood, and played softball in the back yard and drank a lot of beer. Can you imagine that? Jimmy Buffett plays to sold-out stadiums to this day. Drunk, sold-out stadiums.

70

John Denver

John was another act produced by Larry Butler. He had already had so many hit records before he even came to Nashville to record. Even before that, some of you old enough might remember Charlie Rich infamously burning the awards certificate at the CMA Awards after John Denver won for "I'm a Country Boy". Obviously, Charlie wasn't pleased, nor were many other country purists.

Larry was producing an album on John at Sound Emporium. Bill Justis was arranging the strings and recording in the big studio while Buzz Cason, Sheri Huffman, Diane Tidwell and I were adding background voices just across the walkway in the smaller studio. They would finish a song in the big studio then send it over to the smaller studio for us to add voices.

It was late in the day and my feet were killing me from standing all day in my cool cowboy boots. OUCH! We were in the control room listening to a playback of "Some Days Are Diamonds" and I am bitchin' about my aching feet. John notices my whining and tells me to sit down on the couch. A little puzzled as to what I thought he'd said, I ask, "Do what?" He tells me again to sit down on the couch, so I did. He squats down, takes off my boots, and proceeds to give me the most amazing foot massage ever! He's really adept at this, he says, because his cook at his ranch in Wyoming is a licensed masseuse and had taught John how to work all the vital spots. It was amazing!

Now, how many people do you know who can say they've gotten a foot massage from John Denver? Not many, I'd say! Anyway, he was such a nice guy and "Some Days Are Diamonds" was another hit for John Denver!

71

England Dan and John Ford Coley

All the stuff I did with England Dan and John Ford Coley was recorded at "The Pond", a quaint little studio owned by Lee Hazen in the outer reaches of Gallatin. It was one of those studios where a person could almost truthfully say, "You just can't get there from here", but this was the studio Kyle Lehning preferred, so that settled that. Dan and John were great guys. We would play some serious ping-pong games on our breaks on the back porch.

Around 1976 or so, we were adding strings to the already recorded tracks in the middle of a big snow storm in Nashville. Hard to believe, huh? Anyway, the seven string players were understandably concerned about the drive. I just happened to have one of those cool "4-wheel drive" Jeeps, so we decided the strings would meet me at Johnny Cash's Studio on Gallatin Road and ride with me in my Jeep. It took two trips, but we all made it.

Kyle always hired the very best, so naturally the Cherry Sisters were on everything. He also insisted on only seven string players, four violins, two violas and one cello, and firmly believed if we only had seven string players we would be getting the best. He must've been correct, because the strings always sounded marvelous! The truth is though, if you've got a great engineer who's not only an engineer but a fantastic musician as well, they can get a great string sound in a mule barn. It might be a little messy, but it'll be a great string sound.

72

Vince Gill

Vince was already a star before he came to Nashville as the lead vocalist on "Let Me Love You Tonight" with Pure Prairie League. He moved to Nashville for good in the early '80s and had one hit after another, including "When I Call Your Name". I used to play golf with Vinnie at Nashville Golf and Athletic Club, which was a joke since he hit the ball twice as far as I did. At least! He became the host of the CMA Awards around 1985 and continued for twelve years, until he decided he'd had enough of it and moved on to other challenges. David Briggs and I were the music directors for the show starting in 1988, so we worked with Vince for many years.

One day in early 1998, I was playing golf with Bob Beckham, Chet Atkins, and Ray Baker at Hillwood Country Club. It had started raining so the lounge was packed with players waiting for the rain to stop. Vince was one of the ones waiting, and he came over to our table and told me he needed me to do an arrangement for him; said Tony Brown would be getting in touch. So I met with Tony, who told me they wanted this Ray

Charles–type arrangement with strings, background voices, etc. The song was one Vince had co-written with Troy Seals called "If You Ever Have Forever in Mind". It turned out great and was a big hit, followed by Vince performing it in LA on the Grammys with me tagging along to make sure it was done exactly like the record.

It's impossible to name something Vince doesn't excel at. He was a great athlete, a particularly great golfer who probably could've played pro golf if he chose to, a great guitarist, great writer, great singer whose vocal range is ridiculous. He sang harmony vocals on so many big records for other artists. I asked him to harmonize on a project I was producing/arranging on a Glen Campbell Christmas album called "Home for the Holidays". He was marvelous, as usual, and it makes perfect sense that he took Glenn Frey's place with the Eagles (in his spare time).

Amy Grant

I arranged the strings on Amy's first big record called "Father's Eyes" when she was recording for Myrrh Records, a Christian contemporary label in the early '70s. Amy went on from that to some major pop hits with Keith Thomas or Brown Bannister producing: "Baby Baby", "Stay for a While", "Every Heartbeat", "Takes a Little Time", and "That's What Love Is For", to name just a few.

She's one of the sweetest, most beautiful people you could ever meet. I think Vince over-married! Vince and Amy performed some of the music at Fred Foster's funeral, and afterward in the reception hall I was complimenting Amy on her performance when one of the string quartet players, David Angel, joined the conversation and mentioned to Amy that she should hear my string quartet arrangement of Roy Orbison's "Pretty Woman". Her eyes got so big and she asked, "You've got a string quartet arrangement of 'Pretty Woman'?" I replied, "Yes, I do." She excitedly told me she wanted it played at her daughter's wedding as she walked down the aisle. It was perfect! Amy is perfect! Vince over-married!

74

Charlie Daniels

I first worked with Charlie when John Richbourg hired me to arrange a session on Joe Simon in the late '60s and Charlie was hired to play electric guitar. On that session we recorded Harlan Howard's "The Chokin' Kind" and it became my first #1 record — an R&B #1 record, at that.

In the late '70s, Charlie hired me to arrange strings on his album "Million Mile Reflections". It was produced by John Boylan, who came in from LA to scout out the small studio at Woodland Studios. John felt like the studio was too dead, so he brought in plywood to completely cover the floors. Anyway, it was a platinum album that I'm very proud of.

Around 1983 Charlie hired me to arrange all his hits for a symphony show he was doing with the Nashville Symphony at the Opry House called the "The Outing". He also wanted me to conduct, wearing tails and the whole bit. Of course my tux jacket was complimented with my Levi's and my cool black cowboys boots, to Charlie's delight. Right before the show, Charlie presented me with a big, black, ten-gallon cowboy hat that we decided I would wear whilst I was conducting. So I'm standing between Charlie's band and the orchestra, and when I make my first conducting movement, my baton knocks my ten-gallon hat into the drum booth. Hits right on top of the cymbals. Great start!

Charlie was always totally unapologetic for his music. During the sold-out concert, an older couple shouted from the audience to turn the music down. Charlie stopped and politely told them that if they didn't like what they were hearing, he would gladly refund their money and they could go out the same door they came in. The crowd loved it! And I love Charlie Daniels for both his music and his political views. And I've still got that black, ten-gallon cowboy hat!

75

Michael Card

My son Mitch introduced me to Michael's music in about 1987. Just a short time later, Norbert Putnam contacted me and Alan Moore about arranging Michael's new album called "The Beginning". I soon discovered that this particular Michael project was like a book from start to finish, each song leading to the next. It's an absolutely marvelously written work! All the tracks were cut in Nashville at Bullitt Recording Studio, then Norbert and Michael decided the orchestra needed to be added in London with the London Symphony at Abbey Road.

Due to a scheduling conflict, Alan was unable to go to London so I was to conduct the symphony on both his charts and mine. Wow, would my dad be proud of me! As I mentioned before in the Norbert Putnam chapter, as we were boarding the airplane I was given an additional song to arrange called "God Will Provide a Lamb". Writing this chart on a crowded airplane with nothing but an arrangers score and a pencil was certainly not the most conducive atmosphere to be creative, but I think it's one of the best charts I've ever written.

So we got to the tune "Lift Up The Suffering Symbol" that Alan arranged. It's an incredible chart, and Alan didn't flinch at all with what he had written. In certain spots he had the trombones and French horns playing this extremely dissonant cluster, and when we first ran through it, the brass section was exclaiming, "That can't be right!" I told them it might be weird, but that's what he wrote so we had to give it a chance. It was marvelous! Chances are you've never heard it, but if perchance you do, you'll hear what I'm talking about. It's just brilliant writing, like painting a portrait.

I was privileged to get to sing with Michael on "In the Wilderness" and "A Face That Shone". I would highly recommend this music to anyone who has impeccable taste, and even to those of you who have no taste at all.

76

Tony Joe White

In 1969, Billy Swan ("I Can Help") asked me to arrange some horns for a Tony Joe White single called "Polk Salad Annie" that he was producing. I'd never heard of Tony Joe at the time, but who cares, it was work. So I met with Billy to go over the chart. Billy had some definite ideas that he wanted the horns to play, so he hummed them to me. I wrote the charts like Billy instructed me to. We did the horns in Bradley's barn in Mount Juliet, and afterward Billy played it for John Richbourg (the famous DJ on WLAC Radio as well as an R&B producer) to get his approval.

John R. listened to it once and asked Billy, "Who wrote those horns?" Billy said, "Bergen White". Then John R. asked Billy, "Did you tell him what to write?" Billy said yes, then John R. told him, "Do 'em again, but let Bergen write what he hears." To explain, I had been working with John R. on several R&B acts, but in particular a Joe Simon #1 R&B record called "The Chokin' Kind" (my first gold record), so John R. believed in what I would write and he advised Billy to trust me.

We did the horns again, this time at RCA. Same players as before:

Don Sheffield and George Tidwell on trumpets, Billy Puett on alto sax, Johnny Duke on tenor sax, and Swarmin' Norm Ray on baritone sax. When Swarmin' Norm saw the title, he jumped up and ran out to his car. He just happened to have a gunny sack full of polk salad in his trunk. Must've been a good sign. It was a big hit for Tony Joe, and we followed it with Tony's "Black and White" LP.

More about Tony: this swamp thing was for real! To talk to Tony was the same as hearing him sing; it was that natural and effortless. He was the same on the golf course and had what he called his "swamp-snap" — a big hook that rolled a long distance. Tony and I used to go on golf trips with Bob Beckham, so we played a lot of golf together, betting and drinking. A lot!

Tony was a great writer who wrote not only "Polk Salad Annie" but also all the songs on his albums. Brook Benton had a big hit with Tony's "Rainy Night in Georgia" that was covered by many artists. Elvis covered "Polk Salad Annie" and Tina Turner recorded a steamy version of "Steamy Windows".

One of Tony's finest songs, though, is one I'm certain you've never heard. It was never published and was recorded only by Tony Joe himself. He and I are not related, but he called us "brothers" anyway, obviously because of the name, but more importantly because we seemed to feel things with a certain undefinable sensitivity. We had a kinship that is difficult to describe. Tony was inspired by a true story to write a song entitled "Auto-man, Auto-man, Bergen White Is the Auto-man". The song is sung tenderly in a way only Tony Joe could sing it. I'm so fortunate to be in possession of the only recording that exists. If you're twenty-one or older and ask really nicely, I'll tell you the story that inspired "Auto-man, Auto-man, Bergen White Is the Auto-man".

77

Buzz Cason

Buzz and Fuzz doing backgrounds for Jimmy Buffett.

Bobby Russell introduced me to Buzz in the late '60s. Buzz had been in LA for quite some time working with Snuff Garrett, singing on sessions, writing, he could do it all. Bobby and I were doing the hit copies in Nashville, but when Buzz came back, the three of us were doing them, as well as some records on our own like "Tennessee" and "Watermelon". Buzz had a big hit early in his career singing "Look for a Star". He was called Gary Miles, and the record was the theme to some horror movie. Buzz and I sang on a pile of hits like "Baby's Got Her Blue Jeans On" by Mel McDaniel, "Some Days Are Diamonds" by John

Denver, the Chipmunks, and a bunch of Jimmy Buffett stuff.

Buzz and I sang so much together in the '70s until the '90s that people jokingly started calling us the "Bergenaires". After a really slow year of sessions (maybe three), we put an ad in "Billboard Magazine" around Christmas saying, "The Bergenaires want to thank you for another wonderful year." We thought it was funny, even if no one else did. We actually considered buying this old, dilapidated half of a bus that had been sitting in a vacant lot in Berry Hill for years. We were thinking we'd get someone to paint "The Bergenaires" on both sides of the bus, then we would haul it to a different studio once a week. We would've thought it was funny even if no one else did, once again.

Buzz and Mac Gayden co-wrote one of the biggest hits ever, "Everlasting Love", which was originally recorded by Robert Knight but then was recorded by so many others, including Gloria Estefan and U2.

One year Buzz signed a publishing deal with Walt Disney Entertainment. When Buzz received a royalty check that was about a fourth of what he thought it should be, Buzz said, "If you can't trust Walt Disney, who can you trust?"

Buzz built the famous Creative Workshop studio in the late '60s, where I often worked with artists like Olivia Newton-John ("Don't Stop Believing"), Roy Orbison, The Oak Ridge Boys, and many more. When Larry Butler asked me to hire the singers to be the Chipmunks, naturally I called Buzz to be Alvin. Naturally!

78

Wynonna Judd

B rent Maher hired me in 2006 to arrange a Christmas album for Wynonna Judd. Everything live: rhythm, strings, a twenty-four voice choir on six secular and six spiritual songs. We recorded at the Sound Kitchen in Cool Springs in Franklin, Tennessee.

We were running through "Santa Claus Is Coming to Town" when Wynonna announced she wanted to add the intro, which few people were even aware of, but was on the early recordings in the '40s. It started with, "Well, I just got back from a lovely trip along the Milky Way …" It was sixteen bars I'd never heard before so, obviously I hadn't written it, but Wynonna was really intent on adding it, so we gave the musicians a break and I wrote the arrangement. It turned out great, and Wynonna was exactly right to insist on it.

It was a very successful Christmas record called "A Classic Christmas". Wy showed her incredible vocal skills, ranging from "Santa Claus Is Coming to Town" to "Ave Maria" with total ease. I received letters from both Wynonna and her mother, Naomi, telling how much they appreciated the work I'd done. Wynonna was a total pleasure to work with.

Reba McEntire

I worked with Reba from the very beginning of her career when Jerry Kennedy was producing her for Mercury Records. She had some big-time success with Jerry, including "Up, Up, Up to Heaven" that had a big string section and a harp, but as these things happen in this business, she switched from Mercury to MCA Records, with Jimmy Bowen doing the production.

I finally got to work with her again when she switched producers again to Tony Brown. She and Tony were doing a duet CD with lots of acts, including Don Henley and Kenny Chesney, but the one that stood out to me was her duet with Kelly Clarkson on one of Kelly's songs called "Because of You". Kelly had already had a big pop hit on the song. We added a big string section to it, and that was that.

While that record was still out, I was in LA working with Carrie Underwood on the 2007 Grammys when someone snuck up behind me, threw their arms around me, and said, "Guess who!" I had no idea who it was, but it was Reba thanking me for the string arrangement I had done. Reba is a great artist with a very distinctive voice and she's an easy gal to love.

80

Jerry Reed

Jerry was a fabulous guitarist; he was also a writer and actor who had his own style for whatever he was doing. He was the "Snowman" (the semi-truck driver in "Smokey and the Bandit" and the sequel). He co-starred in a movie with Robin Williams as a hit man and was very convincing, to say the least. He was a "hit" man again with records like "When You're Hot, You're Hot" and "Amos Moses" on RCA.

I don't think there is any guitarist Chet Atkins admired more than Jerry Reed. Jerry even had his own weird way of tuning that you'd need to be a guitar player to understand, which I'm not. I'm told though, by those who know, that this tuning was exclusive to Jerry Reed. When I was working with Jerry, I must've kinda let my hair get out of hand, and he appropriately called me the "Vanilla Gorilla". Jerry's wife, Prissy, was an excellent background singer who was the first call to take Anita Kerr's place when Anita retired from the Anita Kerr Singers. Prissy filled that spot until she retired herself.

Jerry was a hoot to play golf with as well; there was never a serious moment with him. Like when I was getting into my putting stance, right before I putt, he would walk to the hole and draw X's in front of it. As if I needed that distraction. Jerry didn't pay any attention to golf rules, or hardly any others, as a matter of fact.

81

Olivia Newton-John

Chris Christian introduced me to Olivia in 1976. She had already had great success with "Have You Never Been Mellow", "Let Me Be There" and "I Honestly Love You", and of course everyone is familiar with the smash musical "Grease" that she co-starred in with John Travolta. "Grease" came out in 1978 and was the highest grossing musical movie in history at that point. Since I worked with her just prior to "Grease", you might argue that I was the one responsible for her getting that gig. That would be wrong, but once it's been said, you can't un-say it.

I suppose when you meet someone who's already had so much success from recordings and movies, you don't expect for them to make you feel like you've known them for years. Olivia was one of those artists that makes you so comfortable, you forget what a famous person they are, and her Australian accent was the cherry on top. Kind of made me want to work a little harder on her stuff, and having Olivia Newton-John on my résumé was cooler than cool!

As I mentioned before, I met her with Chris Christian, at his home studio when I was also meeting with her producer, John Farrar, to talk about the strings for her album "Don't Stop Believing". John and I spoke for a little while discussing some charts I had done that he was particularly fond of, but also making sure I understood that he hated glissandos. His comment was, "There's just got to be another way to build into the chorus." I got his point. Therefore, if you listen to that album you will note the total absence of glissandos!!

82

LeeAnn Womack

I arranged one of LeeAnn's first hits called "The Fool" produced by Mark Wright. She is absolutely one of the finest female artists, in my opinion. She's had so many big records, including "Does My Ring Burn Your Finger?", "Thinking with My Heart", "Stronger Than I Am", "Call Me Crazy", "A Little Past Little Rock", "Something Worth Leavin' For", all the way up to her biggest recording, "I Hope You Dance".

After the phenomenal success of "I Hope You Dance," LeeAnn called me wanting to do a string quartet arrangement of it for a special event she was doing. We discussed the chart over lunch at Princeton's restaurant in Green Hills. I must admit that I would've written the chart for nothing just to have lunch with this gorgeous creature. I also worked with LeeAnn on the Memorial Day and Independence Day concerts in Washington, DC.

83

Neil Diamond

"Cherry Cherry", "Cracklin' Rosie", "America", "Song Sung Blue", "Kentucky Woman", "Brother Love's Travelin' Salvation Show", and is there anyone who can't sing that famous lick on "Sweet Caroline"? These are just a few of Neil's hits.

I've loved Neil's records for years but never got to work with him until Bob Gaudio (of the Four Seasons) produced a CD called "Tennessee Moon" in Nashville. Bob hired me to co-arrange the CD. I met with Bob at Darkhorse Studio to discuss the charts, and while he knew exactly what he wanted, he still gave me a little room to do my thing. Naturally we used Nashville's finest musicians and singers. Everyone wanted to work with Neil Diamond as well as Bob Gaudio.

We recorded the CD at Woodland Studios and then followed with a Neil Diamond special at the Ryman. You would sort of assume these guys would be difficult to work with, given their success, but it was quite the opposite.

Ray Price

In 2010, I worked on a trio CD featuring Willie Nelson, Merle Haggard, and Ray Price called "Last of the Breed", produced by Fred Foster. Until that time, I had only seen Ray on some of the awards shows. Then in 2012, Fred hired me to arrange a final album on Ray called "Beauty Is". Kyle Lehning engineered the sessions at Ocean Way in Nashville.

When we had our first meeting, it seemed our biggest problem was finding a place to park Ray's bus. It couldn't be parked at Kyle's because the neighbors would complain, so after much deliberation we finally decided it would be parked in my back driveway. The first morning we met on the bus. Ray started the day like he usually did, with a stiff shot of Jack Daniels. Ever so reluctantly, I joined him. Ha-ha.

Even though Ray was eighty-seven years old, there was still a lot of Ray Price left in that voice. On a few of the final voice overdubs, though, Ray was so weak he had to sit on a stool to sing, and on one of them I had to sit out there with him to make sure he came in at the right place. Ray knew he was struggling and told Fred, "Send Bergen out here with a stick to punch me when it's time to sing." An outstanding artist to the very end!

85

Randy Goodrum

I had arranged a rhythm session for Larnelle Harris in the mid '70s, and we were cutting tracks and would add the orchestra afterward. I found out a few hours before the session that the piano player I'd hired was ill and couldn't make the gig. However, he enthusiastically recommended I get Randy Goodrum to take his place. Randy was Jerry Reed's keyboard player at the time and conveniently was in town. I must admit I was skeptical since these charts were a bit intricate with all these syncopations, etc., and I'd never worked with Randy. I had absolutely no idea what a fabulous musician he was. He sat down and played these first time through as if he had written them himself. Wow!

In 1978, Brent Maher and Steve Gibson called me to arrange the strings on a Michael Johnson record called "Bluer Than Blue". It was written by, guess who, Randy Goodrum. Michael marvelously interpreted the song but was actually just trying to ape Randy's demo. If you'd heard Randy's demo you would understand why. "Bluer Than Blue" was a big record for Michael and was the fifth single ever released on EMI America Records. I wonder if the first four did as well?

Randy would go on to write "Foolish Heart" and "Oh Sherrie" for Steve Perry and Journey, "You Needed Me" for Anne Murray, "20-20" for George Benson, "Anna" for Toto, "If She Would've Been Faithful" for Chicago, "Power" for Kansas, "It's Sad to Belong" for England Dan and John Ford Coley, to name just a few.

86

The Statler Brothers

I worked on many big records with the Statlers, all with Jerry Kennedy producing. I remember a big crowd of us piling onto a chartered bus to go to Tennessee Tech University in Cookeville to see a Statlers concert with Reba McEntire opening. When I started working with the group, Jimmy Fortune had taken over the tenor spot from Lew DeWitt, who had retired due to illness. All of them were great guys, gracious enough to send me an autographed letter thanking me for my work on one of their Christmas records.

    On one occasion they had done a song called "Charlotte's Web" from the cartoon series. At the very end of the song, there was this six-beat triplet lick that finished off the tune. It was supposed to be played on an accordion, so Jerry had hired this famous accordion player from this equally famous bluegrass family. Anyway, the player arrives at the studio and we think, "This is gonna be a breeze." Well, think again! He finally, after many attempts, requests that Jerry give him the tape so he can take it home and rehearse it.

    Problem was, Jerry was supposed to mix it immediately, so that was not gonna work. So I wound up playing the lick on a B3 organ with the accordion stop pulled out. This lick had eighteen notes, and it took me three tracks to play it, with the track at half speed, six notes at a time. Hey, whatever works; it's show biness!

87

The Gatlin Brothers

Back in the '70s and '80s there was no finer group than the Gatlin Brothers. Larry, Steve, and Rudy had one big record after another. Larry always sang the lead, Steve the low part, and Rudy the high part. I was fortunate enough to work with them on their "Houston" album that Rick Hall produced.

Larry was as fine a writer as he was a singer and wrote all the songs they recorded. He was another great writer from the stable of Bob Beckham. "Broken Lady", "All the Gold in California", "Houston", "I've Done Enough Dying Today", "Denver", "I Just Wish You Were Someone I Love", and the list goes on and on. I had actually pretty much forgotten how many hits they'd had until Steve called in late 2020 asking me to update all their symphony charts. Amazing stuff! Amazing group!

The Gatlins donated a huge Allen Pipe organ to Woodmont Baptist Church back in the mid '60s. My father was minister of music at the church at that time, and my mother continued to be a member there until she passed away in 2001. My dad and mom were so proud that I actually knew the Gatlin Brothers.

88

Barbara Mandrell

"Babs" was one of the cutest, sassiest, most ridiculously talented artists you could ever hope to meet. Tom Collins produced her stuff and had one hit after another: "Sleeping Single in a Double Bed", "If Lovin' Him Is Wrong, I Don't Wanna Be Right", "Angel in Your Arms", "Only a Lonely Heart Knows", "I Was Country When Country Wasn't Cool", "Woman to Woman", "Fooled by a Feeling", to mention a few.

On one of the many specials we did at Bridgestone Arena, I was in a dressing room going over some stuff with the vivacious KD Lang. Oh wait, did I say vivacious? What I meant to say is, she is an insufferable bitch! She was being as difficult as she always was and I was required by my job to put up with her shit. Anyway, whilst I'm miserable with her, I am told on my headset that someone is waiting in the hall to see me. They had to wait at least another half hour for me to finish and when I walked out the door, Barbara was waiting just to give me a hug and say hello since we hadn't seen each other for a while. It was such a marvelous contrast to go from KD Lang to Barbara Mandrell.

She could sing and play almost any instrument you put in front of her, as was witnessed on her weekly TV show, "The Barbara Mandrell Hour", with her sisters, Louise and Erline. She was seriously one of the most talented artists I ever worked with.

89

Wayne Newton

Wayne was another exceptional artist that Larry Butler produced. He flew into Nashville on his private plane. All the musicians and singers were gathered at Eleven-Eleven Sound, and Larry introduced us to Wayne. I had just seen one of the James Bond movies ("License to Kill" with Timothy Dalton) that Wayne was a villain in. He was a much larger man than I expected, and a fantastic actor.

He could not have been more pleasant to be around. The first thing he did was count how many musicians and singers were there, then sent his pilot back to Wyoming to his ranch to bring back all these cool black jackets with an eagle on the back as gifts for all of us. My mother and niece were big fans, so they came to one of the sessions and got their picture made with Wayne and he was gracious and attentive the entire time. That meant a lot to me.

The album we worked on is called "Coming Home" and it's a wonderfully diverse project. The song I remember the most was a duet with the Queen of Country Music herself, Tammy Wynette, and was called, "While the Feeling's Good". That was the biggest hit on the record and I've still got that cool jacket .... Nothing but great memories with Wayne.

Standing from left: David Briggs, Bobby Ogdin, Billy Sanford, Larry Butler, Wayne, Bob Wray, Jimmy Capps and Jerry Carrigan. Kneeling from left Pete Wade, me and James Stroud.

90

Clint Black

One night I'm fast asleep when the phone wakes me up at midnight. I answer and it's Mark Wright. He says, "Hey, man, did I wake you? Hope not. I need you for a session." I say, "Sure, Mark, when is it?" He says, "Right now. Can you come right now?" and then he adds, "Call Jana and see if she can get here."

So I called Jana King, whom I've mentioned before and has her own chapter in the Singers section. I picked her up and arrived about 1 a.m. at Woodland Studio, where Mark and James Stroud were producing Clint Black. They needed us to sing on "Killin' Time", which became an enormous hit for Clint.

In 1996, like the fool that I am, I got married for the fifth time. Right around that time I was doing the CMA Awards and producer Walter C. Miller had made sure everyone on both sides of the Pecos River was aware that I'd gotten married for the fifth time. Clint Black was nominated for just about everything that year, and of course, he too knew about my fifth marriage.

So Clint and his band were on stage, ready for their rehearsal and when I walked out on stage, Clint led his band playing the "Fifth of Beethoven". Clint and Walter thought it was really funny. So did everyone else except me, since I was already trying to get a divorce. Seriously!

91

Little Jimmy Dickens

I can't remember the year, but Little Jimmy Dickens was doing a spot on the CMA Awards. I also can't remember the song he was doing, but as usual we had pre-recorded the track for Jimmy to sing to. The problem for Jimmy, and for us as well, was Jimmy was used to performing his concerts live with his band, and they would follow him, even if he came in in the wrong place. Well, when you've got pre-recorded tracks, that just won't work.

We're starting Jimmy's rehearsal and find out very quickly that Jimmy is having all kinds of trouble singing with this pre-recorded track. So Walter sends me out on stage to help Jimmy come in at the right place. After two or three attempts, with the frustration building, I notice a big tear coming out from under Jimmy's big sunglasses, so I contact Walter to tell him this is simply not going to work.

He agreed, so we wound up with the house band in the back studio following Jimmy on the big screen. It worked very well, so now there was a big Jimmy Dickens smile behind those big sunglasses.

92

The Imperials

I worked with Charlie Tallent on an Imperials album back in the early '70s when the group consisted of Armond Morales, Jim Murray, Dave Will, and Terry Blackwood. We cut the tracks and vocals at Jack Clement Sound, but for reasons I can't remember, we went to LA to add the strings and horns.

Then in the late '70s or early '80s, I was hired to produce and arrange a Christmas project on the group. I had never heard of Russ Taff at the time, but he had joined the group shortly before we started working on the LP. What a marvelous vocalist he was, and still is. He had a very distinctive sound; you knew immediately it was Russ when he sang, and when you surround him with Armond, Jim, and David, how can you miss?

I met with the group to discuss the songs we were going to do. Some of them were new Christmas songs, and some were standards. The label, Myrrh Records, had specified certain songs they wanted to be included, specifically "What Child Is This?". I told the guys, "I've arranged this song so many times I can't imagine doing it again without just repeating one of my earlier charts." Armond told me they had performed it on the road with a sort of jazz feel. I asked to hear it, since I was desperate for a new approach. It was definitely different, and I liked it, maybe just because it was different. I added a few things to it, but overall we did it pretty much like they had been doing it, but with the addition of strings and horns.

The album was released, and after a very short time I started receiving hate mail from people saying I had committed blasphemy on this marvelous Christian song, and I was going straight to hell! I would not pass go, I would not collect $200, I would go straight to hell. I'm certain the good Lord has forgiven me for my blasphemous arrangement, and I'm not so sure I wouldn't yield to temptation and do it that way again if given the opportunity. Woe is me!

93

Marijohn Wilkin

Marijohn seated with L to R: Glen Baxter, Ed Bruce and me.

Bill Justis introduced me to Marijohn, who snatched me up immediately after I got into the business to sing in her quartet, The Marijohn Singers. The group consisted of Marijohn, Ed Bruce singing bass, Glenn Baxter singing baritone, and me singing tenor. We were quickly doing sessions, but primarily we were doing the Grand Ole Opry syndicated TV shows from the Ryman Auditorium. Each Saturday we would rehearse for a little while, but not nearly enough time to prepare to sing behind at least six acts in a thirty-minute TV show. When we would arrive at the Ryman, there would be a line of people from the door of the Ryman all the way down to Broadway, then down Broadway past Tootsie's Orchid Lounge. All these people for a thirty-minute show. Amazing!

Over a period of time we sang behind just about every act in the business. On one of the shows Archie Campbell was the host, and the quartet was singing with him on this song called "Friends". When the song ended, Archie pointed at me and announced the birth of my son Mitch, who had been born that very morning. Thanks, Archie!

Marijohn always wanted me to scribble out the number charts for each song as well as what we were going to sing with each act. On one show we were singing with Jim Ed Brown when he stopped the rehearsal to tell us we were singing with too much "vibrat". Of course, we knew he meant "vibrata", but we said nothing until the show started, and when Jim Ed came on, Marijohn whispered to us, "Stop with the fucking vibrat."

Marijohn was also the mother of John Bucky Wilkin, who was Ronny of Ronny & the Daytonas, which had a major pop hit record in 1965 called "Little GTO". Bobby Russell, Buzz Cason, and I were the original Daytonas. Marijohn was also a prolific writer with big hits on "Waterloo" by Stonewall Jackson, "Long Black Veil" by Lefty Frizzell, and "One Day at a Time" by Marilyn Sellars. It was a great way to start my career, working with, and learning from, Marijohn Wilkin.

94

Bobby Lord

Bobby Lord was a pretty big country act in the '60s. He had quite a number of hit records, plus he had a TV show that The Marijohn Singers sang on regularly.

So we're doing this show with Bobby at the Centennial bandshell outdoor theatre. The temperature was a sweltering ninety-five degrees, but in spite of the weather, the place was packed. He had a big record going on at the time, I can't remember the title, but it had Jim Glaser singing the high tenor harmony part on the chorus. When I say high, I mean HIGH! Before Bobby started singing this hit, he announced to the crowd, "When we get to the chorus on this song, I want you to pay particular attention to the guy on the right who's singing the tenor part. Watch the veins in his neck!"

Well, needless to say, that didn't help since I was dying trying to sing this part and now everyone was looking at me instead of Bobby. The song turned into a comedy act with me providing the comedy. Oh well, It's show biness!

95

John Stewart

John was already famous as one of the Kingston Trio, but left the group to do his own thing. The Marijohn Singers worked on several albums with John, with Nick Venet producing at RCA Studio. He always had his squeeze Buffy with him, for inspiration, I suppose. Anyway, he was a great guy, a great writer, and a vocalist with his own style. Interestingly though, his solo stuff sounded nothing like the Kingston Trio.

I'm not sure what I was thinking, but apparently I wore some weird pants to one of the sessions so John called me Bergen "Britches" White. On one of the last tunes we recorded he ended the song by calling out everyone's name who worked on the stuff, and yes, he called me Bergen "Britches" White. I think the album was called "California Bloodlines". We also worked with John on "Cannons in the Rain".

96

Ronny & the Daytonas

In the mid '60s, Bill Justis combined with John "Bucky" Wilkin to record a hot-rod tune Bucky had written called "Little GTO". It was recorded at Fred Foster's studio in downtown Nashville on 7th Avenue. While Bucky insists that Buzz Cason and I were singing on it, neither Buzz nor I remember it. I'm certain Bobby Russell and Johnny McRae were on it, but beyond that, I don't know. I can say with certainty that Bobby Russell and I were the Daytonas on the short tours we did with the Beach Boys, Jan and Dean, The Knickerbockers, Ace Cannon, and many more. The Beach Boys were amazing! They actually sounded just like their records in live performance. This was when Brian Wilson, Carl Wilson, Dennis Wilson, Al Jardine, and Mike Love were touring.

In need of a follow-up recording, Bill took us to Munich, Germany, in December 1966 to record the "Sandy" album. We went to Munich because it was so much cheaper to record in Europe than in the States, and Bill had some connections. Here we are in 1966 wearing cordless headphones — you could walk all over the studio, into the control room, and back into the studio. We still don't have that in the US to this day. Anyway, we were in Munich for two weeks, and it never stopped snowing. I'm not talking about "nose candy"; I'm talking real snow, 106 inches of it. Anyway, we got an extremely nice LP out of it with some of the most beautiful string arrangements I've ever heard from Bill, one of them written in a cab on the way to Trixie-Tone studio. I learned so very much about recording and string arranging from Bill Justis.

One Ronny & the Daytonas story: Bucky signed with RCA to do an LP with Daytona's-type arrangements on famous songs. Just a note here: Bucky had come to the conclusion that a singer had to make a certain face to get the sound he wanted. Where most groups would sing "oohs" and "aahs", we sang, "uh." Yeah, that's right, "uh." "Uh" in harmony is really cool, but you couldn't sing "uh" without making the "face". Go ahead, you try it. Look in the mirror and sing "uh" for about five seconds without making a face. See what I mean?

Anyway, Bucky had invited a certain big name to sing along with us on "Alfie". So we're "uh-ing" along when Bucky stopped us to say we were not all making the face, particularly the big-name guy. Plus, the big-name guy kept cracking jokes, doing impressions, and it was all starting to piss Bucky off. So finally Bucky snapped, and told the big-name guy to either get serious or get out. Well, the biggie disappeared. As a matter of fact, that LP sort of disappeared as well.

If you're curious as to who the big-name is, here are a few clues: he had hit records in the late '60s all the way through the '90s, he is a great singer and comedian, plays piano, and writes and arranges all his stuff. Still wondering? He started in Atlanta, then Nashville doing sessions. Come on! One final clue … "Don't look Ethel." If you haven't figured it out by now, I'm not gonna tell you who it is.

*Seated from left, Larry Butler, John "Bucky" Wilkin and Jerry Carrigan.
Standing from left, me and Buzz Cason.*

97

The Little Dippers

Buddy Killen was producing a session in the early '60s with The Jordanaires and The Anita Kerr Singers as the artists. I can't remember what tune The Jordanaires did, but the tune The Kerr's sang was a song Buddy had written called "Forever". The Kerr's sounded marvelous, and the recording also featured Pete Drake playing his new invention on the steel guitar where he actually sang the word "forever" through some kind of tube attached to the steel.

It was a smash hit, but The Kerr's had no intention of going on the road to promote it, so Buddy had to come up with a quartet. I was still in college, but Gordon Stoker of The Jordanaires advised Buddy to try to get me to be in the group, and I agreed. Buddy also hired Delores Edgin (of The Dinning Sisters), who worked at that time with The Nashville Edition; Glenn Baxter, who would later be with The Marijohn Singers, and a student from MTSU named Emily Gilmore. Buddy called the group "The Little Dippers". Where the hell did that come from?

We rehearsed a lot, but when it came time to hit the road, I decided

I didn't think it was worth it to leave college to go on the road promoting a record we didn't even do. I think Delores dropped out at the same time, so that was the end of The Little Dippers. I never liked being called a "dipper" to begin with. Being called an asshole didn't bother me, but a dipper? No way!

*From left: me, Delores Edgin, Emily Gilmore and Glen Baxter.
Sheet music for the group that never was.*

98

Jim Stephany

Jim Stephany and me. Taken at the Factory at Franklin after attending the Studio Tenn Theatre production of "Frankenstein".

I've known Jim Stephany since time began, but I only really got to know him after we both happened to reconnect at the "Breakfast Club" in 2013. In the early '70s, both Don Tweedy and I were extremely busy. Jim copied all of Tweedy's stuff, while George Tidwell and Joe Layne copied all of mine. Jim was Bobby Goldsboro's tour manager when Goldsboro had the number one hit "Honey". After Goldsboro, he became the tour manager/sound mixer for Ray Stevens.

From the '70s through 2010 or so, Jim and I had no contact at all, but after reconnecting at the "Breakfast Club" we started playing golf and gawking at young women together — all the stuff old fools do just to look cool, without success.

I nicknamed him "J.J.J." which stands for "Jerkin' Jivin' Jimbo". You would have to know him to understand. Actually, Jim is a very talented musician. He even had his own show, regularly appearing semi-annually from the elegant "Men's Room" at Shoney's, but they kept running out of toilet paper. He used to teach golf and snow skiing in Erie, Pennsylvania, his hometown. He has his own TV ad as "the Most Interesting Man in Music City." I'm not so sure!

99

Don Jennings

Don has been a dear friend of mine for more years than I care to admit. He doesn't actually belong in the "artist" category. He doesn't belong in the producer, writer, or singer category either, but we've got to put him somewhere, so for these purposes, let's just call him an artist. His father, Bob Jennings, was a famous DJ at WLAC Radio back in the '50s. I'm not positive, but I think Chet Atkins introduced us in the early '70s.

Don is the "mayor" of Temple Hills Country Club in Franklin, Tennessee. Actually, no such title exists, but that's what he is called out there since they can't think of anything else that's not insulting. We who play golf with him call him "P.C." which stands for "posing cock", because he stands transfixed like a pillar of salt after each shot, as if he's waiting for someone to take his picture. He plays very well for someone without knees. You see, Don is "vertically challenged" and his golf shorts cover his knees. He and I have consumed at least a barrel of Burnette's Vodka over many rounds of golf. He is also a member of the "Breakfast Club".

The Musicians

100

David Briggs

David and me circa 1972 in Muscle Shoals, Alabama.

If I had to pick my favorite musician it would be easy — David Briggs! David came to Nashville from Muscle Shoals with Norbert Putnam, Jerry Carrigan, and Hurshel Wiginton in 1964: the same year I quit teaching school and sashayed into the music business. He quickly became the favorite of a lot of producers such as Fred Foster, Chet Atkins, Harold Shedd, Ron Chancey, Owen and Jerry Bradley, and Tom Collins, to mention a few. They would book their sessions based around when Briggs could do it. He always knew what to play, when to play, and never overplayed, as so many musicians do. (Ask me when I'm highly inebriated and I'll tell you who they are.)

One day I was working at RCA Studios on a 10 a.m. session when Briggs walked in and asked what I was doing at 2 p.m. I told him nothing, and he said he needed me at Woodland Studio to just act like I'm playing bass, a lip synch kinda thing on a Donna Fargo record called "Jacammo" or something like that. I said I would be there. When I arrived, I was told I was supposed to act like I was playing the Wurlitzer piano. David didn't tell me that this was a live "20/20" filming. What did I care since it was total lip synch, which is what I was lead to believe. I'd never heard the record, and found out at the last minute that the intro was on the Wurlitzer piano. I still didn't care since it was total lip synch. There's a full orchestra, rhythm section, and background voices. David counts it off, and I'm sitting there looking cool not playing anything (the Wurlitzer wasn't even turned on), then David says, "Wait, Bergen screwed it up." My uncle called me from Kansas and said, "I seen ya on TV. You screwed it up, didn't ya?"

On another occasion I went to get my hair cut at my barbershop, Le Bon Ton in Hillsboro Village on 21st Avenue South. My hair stylist was a sexy little gal named Donna, and when I got there, I luckily found a parking spot right in front of the shop. I bop in and find that Donna is still working on someone else and says it will be about fifteen minutes, so I walk back out to my shiny new Chevy Astro van, that had been fully customized, and open the door to get a magazine to kill the time, then go back into the shop. Unfortunately, I realize later that I left the car keys in the lock.

After a few minutes, sexy Donna says she's ready for me, so I sit down in the chair and she puts the apron around my neck and we're ready to do the deed. All of a sudden sexy Donna screams, "DID I JUST SEE YOU'RE VAN DRIVE OFF?" I jump out of the chair and take off running toward town on 21st Avenue. I look like Batman with that apron flapping in the breeze. Sexy Donna quickly jumps into her car and picks me up so as to give chase to the thieves. We could see my van in front of

*David Briggs at the House of David.
He's looking like he really hates my arrangement.*

us and were maybe gaining ground.

After we've passed Vanderbilt and are making the turn where 21st becomes Broadway, I see this motorcycle cop sitting on his bike eating a Wendy's cheeseburger. We stop, and I jump out screaming, "There they go, they stole my van. Look! There they go!" He calmly asks, "Have you got your registration on you?" I yell, "It's in the glove compartment of my van! Look, you can still see it!" He says, as if in slow motion, "You … need … to … have … your … registration … on … you." I shout, "Have you got yours on you?" He replies, "They didn't steal my van!"

By this time my van had disappeared into town. So sexy Donna drove me back to the shop where I called my friend Ham Wallace at Capital Chevy. He immediately came over and picked me up in a pickup truck that I drove for at least a month whilst they were "cleansing" my not-so-cool van.

News travels fast on Music Row! David heard the news, and a few days after the incident he called and left a message on my code-a-phone telling me he had my van. He was laughing so hard he could barely finish his message.

I'm thinking that son of a bitch saw me leave my keys in the lock and took it just for the fun of seeing me squirm. So I'm searching for David, even went to his house and looked over the fence to see if my van was hidden in his back yard. Little did I know he was in LA laughing his ass off.

The police found my van about two weeks later on Joe Johnson Street totally screwed up, but the goons were stupid enough to leave my license plate on, enabling the police to identify it. All of that trouble, and I didn't even get a haircut from sexy Donna.

101

Farrell Morris

From left: Curt Allen, Charlie Tallent, Farrell, me and Bill Justis at Jack Clement Recording Studio in mid '70s.

I was fortunate enough to meet Farrell Morris very soon after I got in the business. Bill Justis introduced us. Farrell was the absolute greatest percussionist and added so much to the sessions he worked. If the percussion part was written, he could make it sound better than it looked. But, with Farrell, you didn't even have to have it written out, and most of the time I didn't. I'd just hand him a rhythm part and say, "Play something cool. I'll take credit for it later." He did, and I did. Truthfully, I didn't take credit for it. I just thought it was a funny thing to say.

On one particular session, Chet Atkins was producing Roger

Whitaker, the British dude who'd already had a big hit record called "The Last Farewell". This was a full session at Sound Emporium, and on one tune, I can't remember the title, I had written in this certain spot for Farrell to "play something cool on the pubic drum." Well, of course there is no such drum as a "pubic drum". We all know what "pubic" is, and where to find it. Anyway, Farrell did play something cool in that spot. Roger loved it, and when we were listening to a playback, he went out to look at the chart to see what it was. Well, they could hear him laughing in Liverpool. Chet even thought it was funny, and that's saying something!

I arranged another full session for a well-known gospel singer from a famous gospel family at Woodland Studio. The studio was packed with eager musicians and singers. I was passing out one of the charts and walked up to Farrell, who was standing behind his marimba. He looked at it and asked, "What do you want me to play?" I replied, "Doesn't matter, play anything. This is a real piece of shit!" While I was speaking, Farrell was shaking his head, trying to get me to shut up. The artist was standing right behind me, and heard every word. Oops! Damned percussionists!

After he had retired I begged him to do this one last show with me in Pensacola, Florida, and he finally relented. He brought his wife, Bobbi, with him, and it was the last gig he ever did. I had some of his parts written, but mostly he was just playing "something cool". Really cool! I really miss Farrell Morris!

102

Wayne Moss

I met Wayne Moss early in my career when we were both working the sound-a-likes. Wayne and I hit it off and almost immediately starting working on what would become my album "For Women Only". He's an absolutely marvelous guitarist and writer. Wayne was one of the three guitarists who played that marvelous lick on Roy Orbison's "Pretty Woman". The other two were Jerry Kennedy and Billy Sanford.

Wayne was on almost every session I did for maybe five years, when one day we're doing this session on a kid named Browning Bryant, with Alex Zanetis producing. Wayne told all the musicians after the session that he was done: that he was finished doing recording dates. None of us believed him, but he was serious. He never did another session unless it was at his own studio, Cinderella Sound, in Madison right behind his house.

At RCA Studio, there was a small harpsichord I absolutely loved so I asked where it came from and found out it was a kit you could get from Zuckerman's in New York. Of course I ordered one. Wayne and I picked it up at Union Station and excitedly drove to Cinderella Sound, to put it together. We took all the parts out of the boxes, and they completely covered the floor of the studio. Must've been 8,241 pieces, give-or-take a few. Wayne and I looked at each other and immediately started putting all that shit back in the boxes. I took it to my dad to build and gave him my sixteen-foot runabout boat in a trade. I used the harpsichord on a lot of recordings and still have it sitting in my living room today.

Wayne was a member of the cult-favorite Area Code 615 and also formed Barefoot Jerry, where he wrote and sang all the songs. When we recorded "The Chokin' Kind" on Joe Simon in 1969, Wayne and Charlie McCoy switched instruments. Wayne played bass and Charlie played guitar. It was Wayne who came up with that marvelous bass line. I wish I could say I wrote it, but that wouldn't be true. I think I'll say it anyway.

103

Charlie McCoy

Charlie McCoy is probably one of the finest musicians I've ever known. He can play anything: bass, guitar, trumpet, sax, keyboards, and he's a wizard on harmonica. When I first got in the business I immediately became part of Charlie's band called Charlie McCoy and the Escorts. With them, I played the few notes I remembered on the trombone, some bass, the farfisa (an organ sounding thing), and sang. We were not a country band. We did Motown stuff, and did it extremely well.

I remember many times when we would be doing a Temptations or Four Tops tune, and Wayne Butler and I would be playing trombone, Jerry Tuttle was on sax. Charlie would play bass with his left hand and trumpet with his right hand, and sing. Absolutely amazing! I was having trouble playing the three or four notes on my trombone while Charlie was playing this intricate, fast-moving Motown bass line with his left hand, while playing these complex horn licks with his right. Again, absolutely amazing!

Check out this band: Charlie, Kenneth Buttrey on drums, Mac

Gayden on electric guitar (Mac could fill up the whole room with sound by himself), Wayne Butler and Jerry Tuttle on horns, and me on whatever was left, which wasn't much! I remember one morning we were doing the "Ralph Emery Morning Show" at 6 a.m. We opened the show with the rousing Tom Jones classic "It's Not Unusual". Maybe Ralph thought that was a little too rambunctious for that early in the morning, so then he asked Charlie to play something solo. Charlie played "Last Date" on the piano.

    Charlie worked with just about every act that recorded in Nashville. He was instrumental in getting Bob Dylan to come to Nashville to record. Charlie was hired by just about all the producers, because once again, he could play anything. He could also arrange. That's Charlie's string arrangement on "If It's Not Asking Too Much" from my LP "For Women Only".

104

Bobby Ogdin

I worked with Bobby on so many projects: the fabulous Kenny Rogers and Wynonna Christmas duet "Mary, Did You Know?", "The Bergen White Christmas Singers" CD, Kathie Lee Gifford, and many, many more.

One of the more memorable ones was a custom gig I was called for. We called them custom if the artist was not signed to any label, but had lots of money and fancied themselves as recording artists. I cannot remember the artist's name, which is just as well, but he had sent me two or three songs he wanted me to arrange and handle the sessions — money was no object; he had plenty.

So I hired all my favorite players and singers (including Bobby as leader) and told them to keep a straight face during this session. I warned them because the main song was titled "Jalapeño Lips". The lyrics to the chorus were "Jalapeño lips, tortilla chips, holy guacamole, blessa my souly, I love you." I'm dead serious! These ridiculous lyrics were what the background singers had to try to sing without rolling on the floor in hysterics. Somehow they managed to do it!

When the session was done with no casualties, we all went on our merry way. About six months later I walked into Woodland Studios, went to the snack bar to get a cup of coffee, and on the bulletin board was a review from "Record World Magazine" by Robert K. Oermann, enlarged about twenty times. It almost covered the entire bulletin board. It read "'Jalapeño Lips', produced and arranged by Bergen White" and continued, "Possibly the worst rhyme scheme in the history of recorded music!"

And to think I used to bitch about not getting label credit. Here was a time when I would've begged not to get it, but got it anyway. Bobby had gone all over town putting this review on the bulletin boards. "Jalapeño Lips" could be the reason my producing career never flourished. Keyboard players could be another reason. Oh well.

105

Shane Keister

Shane played piano like my parents wanted me to play piano; that's why they made me take piano lessons when I was seven years old. It was only for a year, but seemed like ten. I refused to practice. I was already an asshole at seven years of age.

Anyway, back to Shane. His last name is Keister, pronounced *Keester*, so I nicknamed him "Meester Keester". He was a marvelous pianist as well as arranger. I worked with Shane so much that he knew what I wanted to hear, so he played it. Shane was at the piano on all the stuff I did with Glen Campbell, the live Christmas album called "Home for the Holidays", and the Christian contemporary album called "Show Me Your Way".

One particular experience with Shane: Glen had a cassette copy of Jimmy Webb playing piano on a classic Christian song called "I Will Arise and Go to Jesus" with some really tasty chord changes. Glen wanted to do it exactly like Jimmy did, so he gave the cassette to Shane when he arrived at Eleven-Eleven Sound.

Glen had a few vocal overdubs to do, so Shane had a few minutes to listen to the cassette. When we were ready for Shane, he sat down at the piano and played it, solo, exactly like Jimmy had played it, in the first take. Remarkable! Glen added his voice, I arranged the strings and the Boys Choir of Harlem to go with it, and it was done. It was just another session for Shane, but it was very special to me. I highly recommend you to check it out on Google or YouTube!

106

Larry Hall

Back in the mid 70's, synthesizers were new and many synth players were trying to take the place of string sections. It was forbidden by the Union for producers to hire these people simply because it was putting string players out of work. Well, most producers didn't give a shit as long as they could save money and get away with it. The Union finally gave up on trying to fight it, so here we are in 2021 and I, of all people, am singing the praises of one of these synth guys. Larry Hall is as fine a musician as I've ever worked with, yet I've never been in the studio with him.

I've been honored to arrange for the National Symphony Orchestra for the Memorial Day and Independence Day concerts for the last twenty-or-so years. They finally decided they needed scratch tracks (mock or demo tracks) so the artists could hear what the arrangement sounded like for each show, so I hired Larry to do them. Well, let me tell you, the National Symphony Orchestra doesn't sound as good as Larry's scratch tracks. This is Larry performing all the parts, from the top violins to the arco basses, including all the woodwinds, brass, percussion, harp and choir, the whole thing on his synth. It is absolutely amazing!

On a project I co-produced with Kyle Lehning on Randy Travis, that had a full orchestra, Larry delivered it all on synth and I would defy anyone to be able to tell the difference between Larry and the real thing. And he's a marvelous arranger and singer as well! What an insufferable asshole! HaHa! He's been Ronnie Milsap's band leader and keyboardist for quite a while and I can assure you, if Ronnie Milsap uses him, then he must be the best! I agree, he is!

Larry and me at New Hope Church Auditorium recording the ambiance for the Randy Travis CD "This Never Happened".

107

Steve Gibson

I was made aware of Steve, by my dear friend Buzz Cason, who was using Steve on his demo sessions in the early '70s. He didn't stay a demo musician for very long, as producers quickly started wanting him for their master sessions. Kyle Lehning was using Steve on all the hits with England Dan and John Ford Coley back in the mid '70s to early '80s: "I'd Really Love to See You Tonight", "Nights Are Forever Without You", and "Love Is the Answer", to name a few.

I worked with Steve on so many Jim Ed Norman projects, the Jon Secada "Classics" CD, and the Willie Nelson/Ray Price projects with Fred Foster. Steve co-produced with Brent Maher the Michael Johnson mega hit "Bluer Than Blue" that I was honored to arrange the strings for. I also added strings to the "Engelbert Humperdinck" CD that Steve produced. Steve is still working sessions and is currently the music director for the CMA Awards.

108

Kenneth Buttrey

Kenny was the first really great drummer I ever worked with. He was in Charlie McCoy and the Escorts, as well as being one of the most in-demand session drummers. He legitimately earned the nickname "Buffalo" because musicians didn't dare rush or drag if Kenny was the drummer. Naturally, Kenny played on my LP "For Women Only".

As in demand as Kenny was for sessions, he made the difficult choice of going on the road with Linda Ronstadt, even though everyone tried to talk him out of it. A musician who has been accepted as one of the very best session drummers puts all that on hold to go on the road? I'm sure he was made an offer that he felt he couldn't refuse and might've enjoyed the road, but after a few years of it, when he came back to town, everything had changed. Unfortunately, he never got back to where he was before.

Even more unfortunate, though, Kenny was diagnosed with cancer and we lost him way too soon. The "Buffalo" made a lasting impression.

109

John Willis

John is one of those rare guitarists who can play both rhythm and electric lead guitar with ease. I never put a chart in front of John that he couldn't play, he just knew how to make it work.

He was my first call for rhythm guitar. When David Briggs and I were doing the CMA Awards, John was always our guy. He played both rhythm and electric on my "The Bergen White Christmas Singers" CD in 1999. He also played both rhythm and electric on the Kenny Rogers "Classic Love Songs" triple CDs that Jim McKell and I produced in 1996. John was with me on the Jon Secada "Classics" CD and the Willie Nelson/Ray Price projects produced by Fred Foster.

For the concerts we did at the Kennedy Center in Washington DC, honoring Roy Acuff and Johnny Cash, John was the rhythm guitarist. You simply could not go wrong with John Willis!

110

Jim Isbell

"Izzy" is what I call Jim Isbell. The nickname has no particular significance except it's what I call him. He was a great drummer whose credits include the Neon Philharmonic's "Morning Girl" and "I Love Peanut Butter" by the Newbeats, among many others. He came from Biscayne Island, Florida, and moved to Nashville about the same time as Charlie McCoy, and immediately started working sessions. He actually survived being on the road with Jerry Lee Lewis, and the stories he tells would have you rolling on the floor in laughter.

Jim, Ronnie Gant, and I took many golf trips with Bob Beckham. Izzy's one-liners are historic. It's one of those things where you kinda had to be there to understand. One day one of us was bitching about a shot that we'd just knocked out of bounds and Jimmy said, "You know, that ball goes exactly where you hit it." Let that sink in for a moment …. Is that comment helpful in some way? Maybe you have to be a shitty golfer to think that's funny. I thought it was hilarious. When Jimmy had a forty-foot putt and hit it only twenty feet, he said, "That would've been a great putt if the hole had been right there," pointing at where his ball stopped. "Yogi" Isbell!

On another golf trip, this time to Dancing Rabbit Golf Course in Philadelphia, Mississippi, Jimmy and I were choking to death in the back of the van while Richard Eller and Bob Beckham were chain-smoking in the front. Jimmy waved his hand in front of his face to clear the smoke, looked at me, and said, "I just got a new TV", then asked, "Have you got one?" Let that sink in for another moment …. We're not talking about a Maserati; we're talking about a TV.

On another one of our trips to Palm Springs with Richard and Beckham, Jimmy and I were sharing a condo. Each night while we were watching TV, Jimmy would be playing these little drum licks and betting with me that I could or could not identify the records. From the drum licks, mind you. He thought it was hilarious that I couldn't identify any of them. Presumptuous asshole!

111

Jim Horn

Jim Horn, me, David Briggs and Larrie Londin in Detroit for the show "This Coutry's Rockin'".

One day Jim, Don Sheffield, and I were having lunch at the Green Hills Grille. We were in the midst of riveting conversation, but I was distracted by the song that was being piped through the speakers; it was "California Dreamin'" by the Mamas and the Papas. When the music got to the flute solo I couldn't help myself and I said, "Damn, don't you know that flute guy wishes he'd had another shot at that?" Sheffield started laughing hysterically while Jim started making all these excuses about the flute part. I had absolutely no idea it was Jim playing that flute. He claimed he actually only had one shot at it, even though he begged for more.

Kinda like me and Don Gant with "Lucille", the producer's opinion is the only one that matters. Actually, my comment about that flute part, even though it was unintentional, got Jim back for a comment he had made that was repeated to me about my "shitty" horns on "Polk Salad Annie".

When I was recording my "The Bergen White Christmas Singers" CD with Owen and Jerry Bradley, I brought Jim in to add the flute and sax parts. On "Rockin' Around the Christmas Tree" Jim played the sax solo that Boots Randolph had made famous years earlier. In one take! Why do it again? It was perfect.

I was having a drink with Jim one day and he said, "Hey, man, I heard your van was stolen." I replied, "Yeah, Briggs called claiming he stole it and was laughing his ass off." Jim said, "Oh no, he didn't! Wow, what an asshole!" I found out later that Jim had been with David, urging him on when he called claiming he stole it. And these are my friends?

Jim's résumé borders on the absurd. It would take less time to mention artists he didn't work with than artists he did work with. The Mamas and the Papas, Steely Dan, Elton John, The Beatles, Elvis, The Beach Boys, Boz Scaggs, Linda Ronstadt, and John Denver are a few just to give you an idea. All of those were before he moved to Nashville, and then he worked with everyone here. I used him anytime I got the slightest chance. Jim is another one of those fabulous musicians who knows what to play, and when to play it.

112

Larrie Londin

L arrie brought such energy to whatever session he was doing. Drummers should be the leaders, and a leader he certainly was. I loved working with Larrie! One year David Briggs was hiring a band for a show to be done in Detroit called "This Country's Rockin'". David hired a fantastic group of musicians, with Larrie as the drummer. Not only was he a great drummer, but he was also an expert in karate, so you didn't want to get on his bad side. He was always so jovial, cracking jokes, but underneath all that good humor was a beast.

Anyway, we were on stage about at the end of our rehearsal when Larrie heard asshole Ted Nugent, who was rehearsing next, make the comment, "I'll be out there if we can get these country bumpkins off the stage." Well, we got off the stage, all right, and thought Larrie was gonna kill him. If the stage crew hadn't hurried Nugent onto the stage, it would've gotten extremely ugly.

Just a few years later, Larrie was doing a drum seminar somewhere in Texas and had a massive stroke. We lost him way too soon.

Larrie, George Benson, me and Chet Atkins at Chet's home studio recording Chet and George Benson's CD called "Stay Tuned" in 1983.

113

Reggie Young

Reggie was a marvelous guitarist and one of the easiest guys to get along with. Before he was persuaded by David Briggs to move to Nashville, he played on all those hits that came out of Memphis: B.J. Thomas' "Hooked on a Feeling", Dusty Springfield's "Son of a Preacher Man", Elvis' "Suspicious Minds" and "In the Ghetto", Dobie Gray's "Drift Away". The list is too long to try to cover.

On one cut of mine from my "Finale" CD called "Curious to Know", he played the funkiest guitar you'll hear. I had told him I was going to pitch the song originally to BB King, so he gave me primo BB King, in one take!

I can't remember the year, but Fred Foster hired me to arrange an album on the "Sax King" Boots Randolph. The album featured famous movie themes. One of the songs was from "Roots". In my attempt to imitate Bill Justis, I titled it "Boots Toots Roots". When Reggie saw the music on his stand he almost fell out of his chair laughing. He kept that chart in his guitar case for years.

Reggie, David Hungate, me and David Briggs at a Union meeting in 2013.

114

Mac Gayden

When I first got in the business in 1964, I joined Charlie McCoy and the Escorts. It was truly a remarkable band that specialized in pop and R&B. Mac Gayden was the electric guitarist in that group. When I first heard Mac play I knew there had to be another guitarist playing with him, but no, it was all Mac. He could fill up the entire room with sound, almost always with an R&B edge to it. Mac provided the innovative *wah wah* slide technique on J.J. Cale's hit "Crazy Mama". Mac performed on my 1969 album "For Women Only", because I only hired the best, doncha know.

In addition to being a marvelous musician, he was just as amazing as a writer, an R&B writer from Nashville! He co-wrote the classic "Everlasting Love" with Buzz Cason, first recorded by Robert Knight, but then covered by so many artists, including Gloria Estefan, U2, Natalie Cole, and many more. Mac was a member of the cult-favorite band Area Code 615, as well as Barefoot Jerry, and had his own touring group called Skyboat.

115

Clayton Ivey

If I could play piano, I'd want to play like Clayton does. When I'm writing string or horn charts, I always love to sneak in those little notes that no one would expect, much like Clayton does when he's playing piano, but he does it much better.

In the early '80s, I was arranging a session for Chet Atkins produced by David Hungate, and Clayton was the keyboardist. The tracks had already been cut, and I was adding strings and horns to them. I cannot remember the specific song, but Clayton played the absolute coolest chord changes I'd heard in a long time. The chords themselves were not that unique, but with Clayton adding his "thing" to them they were fantastic. Really simple for him, but opened up a whole new set of possibilities for me. I actually wrote a song based on these chords he played. It was called "Lido Ladies" and was recorded by my friend Jim Horn on his "Neon Nights" album that became a #1 easy-listening jazz recording.

Clayton came from Pensacola, Florida, but has now relocated to Muscle Shoals, Alabama, with his wife, the incomparable Lisa Silver.

What a team they make. My wives, it seemed, were always on a different team. Dammit! I tried hard enough though! Well, I don't know, do you think five times is enough?

116

Henry Strzelecki

Henry and I at Millie Kirkham's 90th birthday party at Richland Country Club around 2010.

It seemed like Henry was on almost every session I worked when I first got in the business. Upright or electric bass . . . he was a master. Henry had the very best attitude, and he was always the same. You knew what to expect from Henry, and you got it each time. Being able to work with him from the beginning when I had zero experience in the studio was a godsend for me. He was always so upbeat and encouraging, it was easy to see why he was in such demand.

In the mid '70s, Simon and Garfunkel booked Columbia's big studio for an entire week and naturally, Henry was hired to play bass. It was not unusual for these sessions to go into the middle of the night, so on one occasion at about 2 a.m., the duo and the band were relaxing, chatting etc. Straight out-of-the-blue Henry asks, "Whatever made you guys come up with the name Gar-funk-el?", with emphasis on each syllable. Time seemed to stand still as the band was staring at each other in disbelief that Henry asked the question. Art looked at Simon and replied, "Well, it wasn't that difficult a decision since my family name is Garfunkel!" The band was in hysterics and after a bit of a pause, Henry sheepishly said "Oh."

Chet Atkins would hardly work without Henry, and that speaks to how good he was. The last time I saw Henry was around 2010 at Millie Kirkham's 90th birthday party at Richland Country Club. Only a few years after that he was run over by a drunken neighbor and died three days later. Henry was a winner, to say the least!

117

George Tidwell

Bill Justis introduced me to George in 1965 or 1966. He was a marvelous copyist and played a mean trumpet, and was also from Memphis, as was Bill. He was my first copyist until he was so busy he couldn't handle the amount of work I was needing, so he introduced me to Joe Layne, who became my copyist for the next maybe twenty years. At that time all the copying was done by hand.

George helped me so much in those early days with his sage advice about writing for horns. He's the one who told me for R&B charts it would be good to overlap the horns. First trumpet on top, alto sax next, second trumpet, tenor sax, and baritone sax on the bottom. I used that voicing on both "The Chokin' Kind" and "Polk Salad Annie". George was also in both of those horn sections with Don Sheffield, Johnny Duke, Billy Puett, and Norm Ray.

I still use that voicing to this very day for that type of chart. I always struggled with the voicing on "raised nine" chords until George filled me in. He was also an accomplished arranger himself, so it was extra cool that he would share his secrets with me.

118

Don Sheffield

Don was the lip trumpet dude when I first started arranging. "Lip" meaning he always played the high trumpet part. He was on every session I did in those early years that had horns.

He used to be Boots Randolph's band leader on the road, and let me tell you, hearing "Yakety Sax" every night can really take its toll. Maybe it kind of explains what's wrong with him now. Don had a not-so-hidden ambition to be a stand-up comic. He thought he was Henny Youngman or Jackie Mason. He practiced all his material on me until he realized my snoring was louder than his jokes. Normally when Don calls I need to check my watch to see how much time I have to listen to one-liners. Some of them are actually funny!

119

Paul Leim

L ike Jim Horn, Paul worked for just about everyone in LA before deciding to bring his expertise to Nashville. He's an absolute magician with a drum set.

Actually, I first got to work with Paul on many of the Christmas albums that Jim Ed Norman produced for Warner Bros. As I mentioned earlier, on so many of these recordings the music would never stop after the first downbeat. Jim Ed wanted orchestral segues between each tune. Sounds simple? Wrong! For example, let's say we're going from "Santa Claus Is Coming to Town" to "What Child Is This?". Different tempos, different moods, different everything, so how do you seamlessly get from 140 beats a minute to 88 beats a minute? Paul Leim! I would be conducting the orchestra, but Paul is the one who got us into the different tempos. Sometimes the segue itself had tempo changes. I would be waving my arms around like Arturo Toscanini trying to conduct, but no one was paying any attention to me because everyone was following Paul. I took credit for all of it, but no one believed me.

I worked with Paul on so many projects, including the Glen Campbell contemporary Christian CD called "Show Me Your Way" and Glen's live Christmas CD called "Home for the Holidays".

120

Billy Sanford

Billy's beginnings were quite modest. He was the lead guitarist in Roy Orbison's band! How modest is that? He's one of the three guitarists who played that famous guitar lick on "Pretty Woman"; the others were Jerry Kennedy and Wayne Moss.

I worked many sessions with Billy. I'll never forget when we were leaving the studio for a lunch break behind Columbia Studios he would throw his Stratocaster like a Frisby into the parking lot. He did it over and over, but then he would play it on the next session. I think it might've improved the sound!

He was a great player who always brought the best attitude as well as talent to the studio. When my wife Carole died in a car wreck in 1983, my dear friend Ron Chancey picked me up to take me to the funeral home in Columbia, Tennessee. I'll never forget when we got to the funeral home Billy Sanford and Bobby Wood were there waiting for me. That kind of thing sticks with you.

121

Beegie Adair

Beegie is a classically trained pianist who specializes in jazz and is one of the finest I've ever heard. She can play anything with such ease it almost pisses you off that something that good could be so easy. She played on both of my albums, and on "Finale" she plays this gorgeous forty-second intro into "Billy You're My Friend" that is absolutely perfect!

When we were recording my album at Jack Clement Recording Studio, she walked in and listened to the cut one time, then sat down at the piano and played this incredible intro. One take! I cannot tell you how many people have complimented me or asked if it was me playing. Well, I'll tell you the truth, I would shave off my left testicle to be able to play that. Or maybe my right, I don't know, but that's a lot to give ... Wait a minute, I lost my train of thought.

Beegie is amazing! I'm not even sure she remembers playing on that song since it was so easy for her. Next time someone asks me, I think I'll just go ahead and say I played it. Maybe not, though, because then they might ask me to play it again. If they do, I'll tell them to kindly kiss my ass!

122

Michael Rhodes

If you've ever seen any of the Joe Bonamassa specials, then you've seen Michael Rhodes playing bass. He's the tall, thin dude with the shaved head, always wearing black, hard to miss. Needless to say, he's an excellent musician!

Michael used to call me "Bergemeister" and presented me with a yellow rubber chicken that when you squeezed it hard enough, it made this extremely loud clucking sound so as to get the attention of cantankerous musicians who loved to ignore me. I've still got that chicken, but there's no one around to ignore me. Bummer!

He was a member of the house band for the CMA Awards shows when we could get him. I used him on my "Finale" project playing on "Curious to Know" and "Lookout Mountain". Michael knows when to play and what to play, an absolute master on the instrument!

123

Grady Martin

When I first got into the music business in the mid '60s, Grady was working three to four sessions a day as a member of the A-Team. Producers booked their sessions around Grady's availability. He played that marvelous acoustic guitar on Marty Robbins "El Paso", the lead guitar on Loretta Lynn's "Coal Miner's Daughter", and Sammi Smith's "Help Me Make It Through the Night", as well as too many other big hits to mention.

In Grady's later years, Fred Foster was producing an album on him featuring famous western movie themes like "High Noon". We had already recorded the rhythm tracks and were now adding a big string section. The control room at Creative Workshop was packed with visitors; many students and teachers from Middle Tennessee State University wanting to witness a live recording session.

One of the tunes was "The Last Roundup", popularized by Bing Crosby in the '40s, but recorded by just about every artist who ever did a western recording. (If you remember Bing Crosby, you're as old as I am, but enough about that.) The lyrics to the chorus were, "Get along little dogies, get along, get along, get along little dogies get along." I got this zany idea that I thought it would be funny if the string players all stood up and started singing the chorus instead of playing it. I whispered to Shelly Kurland (the string contractor) to ask the players to go along with it. They all agreed, even though some were not too thrilled about it. The fact is, 99.9 percent of session string players were formerly symphony musicians — generally considered to be a bit aloof, no nonsense. Well, what transpired on this session totally dispelled that notion.

When it got to the chorus, all the players stood and started singing, "Get along little dogies." The control room erupted in laughter, and Grady thought it was hilarious. Fred was sound asleep, so he missed the whole thing.

124

Ray Edenton

Ray was one of the original A-Team members. He was as steady a rhythm player as you could ever find. He was always very supportive of me when I was first starting and almost seemed an unwilling participant when the A-team was "initiating" me on the Willie Nelson session in 1969.

One day at RCA Studios we had a full session with rhythm, big string section, background voices, the whole thing. Ray had hired everyone, including me to arrange the stuff. All the musicians had filed into the studio and were warming up when Ray decided to introduce everyone to the artist, whose name I cannot remember. He wasn't a famous act, just someone who had a lot of money and thought he could sing. Ray finally got around to introducing me and he said, "This is the arranger."

We ran through the first song, and then the artist came over to me and asked, "Which park do you work in?" Puzzled, I said, "Excuse me?" He repeated his question: "Which park do you work in?" Ray heard this and almost died laughing. He finally jumped up and explained, "No, no, no, he's not a park ranger, he's a music arranger." The way that session turned out, maybe I should've been working in the parks.

The Singers

125

The Cherry Sisters

In the early '70s I was at a session at Audio Media Studios on 19th Avenue South. To be honest, I can't remember why I was there, or who was producing the session, but I do remember hearing this angelic trio: Sheri Huffman, Diane Tidwell, and Lisa Silver. I already knew all of them, but had never heard them sing together. They were absolutely sublime. They provided the background vocals on so many hits in the '70s and '80s: England Dan and John Ford Coley, Dr. Hook, B.J. Thomas, Kenny Rogers, Lee Greenwood, Ronnie Milsap, Bill Medley, Randy Travis, Ray Stevens, John Denver, Engelbert Humperdink, Dean Martin, and Con Hunley, among many others.

Anytime I got an opportunity, I would hire them. Why wouldn't I? They had it all. They could read (which is so very important to me because I always loved to write the vocal parts), they could fake it, and they were so very pleasant to look at.

I'll never forget one particular session where I had written the charts and the Cherrys were doing their thing. I can't remember who the producer was, which is just as well because he was dumber than a box of rocks. Somewhere along the way he was trying to think of something "producerish" to say so as to look like he was actually producing the record. Since he was babbling incoherently, one of the Cherrys suggested they all switch parts to give it a different sound. He liked that idea, but here's where it all fell apart: the very first thing the Cherrys sang was unison (for those who don't know what that means, *like the producer*, singing "unison" means they were all singing the same part, no harmony).

So the tape starts and the girls start singing unison, he stops it immediately and says, "No, no, no, that won't work." One of the Cherrys tries to explain, "But we're all singing unison." He comes back with, "Doesn't matter, that's not gonna work!" The Cherrys pause, then say, "Okay.", in unison.

The Cherrys gather in town every year in the early summer to spend a few days together and always include Kyle Lehning and me for lunch or dinner. In 1984, the Cherrys had a gala party at my house that included swimming, drinking, dinner, and music. I never had so many people at my house as I did for the "Cherry Jubilee". *Everyone* loved the Cherry Sisters.

Where did the name "The Cherry Sisters" come from, you ask? On a Gene Cotton session in 1975 at Jack Clement Recording Studios, I was privileged to be singing with the Cherrys when Bill Justis walked into the studio and said, "Well, well, if it's not BW and the Cherry Sisters!" The name stuck.

The last time I got to work with the Cherrys was when Kyle Lehning brought the Cherry Sisters and me together again to sing on a Randy Travis Christmas CD called "Songs of the Season". It was absolute magic! It reminded me just how good these gals were. I could go on and on about them ad nauseum, but suffice it to say, I loved the Cherry Sisters, and still do.

The Singers: The Cherry Sisters

Sheri Huffman, Lisa Silver and Diane Tidwell.

126

Gordon Stoker/The Jordanaires

Gordon Stoker was the leader of the Jordanaires and was also a dear friend of my father. They both attended Oklahoma Baptist University when I was about seven years old, so I've known him just about all my life. I fondly remember Gordon and his lovely wife, Jean, taking my sister, Barbara, and me to the big Centennial swimming pool when we were in high school. It was so cool since he was a star, working on all of Elvis' early hits, plus just about every act you can think of at the time. Gordon even played piano on some of Elvis' early stuff.

The Jordanaires were on stage with Elvis on the "Ed Sullivan Show". Ricky Nelson's "Travelin' Man" and "Hello Mary Lou", Johnny Horton's "Battle of New Orleans", Tennessee Ernie Ford's "Sixteen Tons", and Jimmy Dean's "Big Bad John" all were backed by the Jordanaires, and I'm not even scratching the surface. When I was first getting into the business, Gordon already knew what I was capable of, so he started using me to fill in if one of them couldn't make a session. He did the same thing with Ray Stevens.

On one of the first sessions when I was filling in, Neal Mathews had scribbled some shape notes on the chart. I whispered to Gordon, "I know those are shape notes, but I haven't seen them since I was a little boy in a Baptist hymnbook." So, Neal wrote the numbers for me.

Filling in with the Jordanaires was great for my ever-growing résumé, and without a doubt, Gordon was instrumental in so many opportunities that fell my way. The evening I met Elvis for the only time was all because Gordon couldn't get in touch with Neal Mathews, so he called me to fill in. Talk about being in the right place at the right time!

127

The Nashville Edition

In the roaring '60s, '70s, and '80s there were three background singing groups that worked on at least seventy-five percent of all the recording done at that time: The Jordanaires, The Anita Kerr Singers, and The Nashville Edition. The Nashville Edition included Hurshel Wiginton on bass, Ricky Page on soprano, Delores Edgin on alto, and Joe Babcock on tenor. When Ricky Page moved to LA, Wendy Suits came in as the soprano. Of the three groups, The Kerrs had the slickest sound, whereas The Jordanaires and The Nashville Edition offered pretty much the same thing, except The Jordanaires were an all-male quartet, and The Edition was mixed. All three groups were equally excellent at coming up with great ideas for arrangements and doing them fast, since in those days you were trying to record at least three songs, many times four songs, in a three-hour session.

A funny little story about Joe Babcock, actually Joe's wife, Joyce. I was in my car one afternoon listening to WKDA radio, and this disk jockey was having a little contest with his listeners. He would call a listener, and if the listener answered saying, "WKDA", they would win a prize. The DJ said he was calling one of the entries, Joyce Babcock. You heard the phone ringing and she answered with, "Hello", and the DJ said, "Oh no, Joyce, you should've answered WKDA, but thanks for entering."

Joyce was very disappointed, to say the least, and hung up. Well, I just happened to have Joe's home number so I called Joyce right back and she answered, "Hello", and I said, "Oh no, Joyce, you've done it again." There was absolute silence on the other end of the phone. I'm not sure Joyce was very amused, but Joe and I laughed about it a lot.

128

Jana King Evans

I worked so much with Jana when she first came to town, and I'm sure I would still be working with her if she hadn't fallen in love and left town with that scoundrel Dennis Evans. She was another of those wonderful vocalists who could sing anything. She could read, she could fake it, she could write the charts herself, almost made me question why I was even there to begin with. For any of you who might've been fans of the Ralph Emery–hosted show "Nashville Now", she was the cutie brunette standing on the left side of the background vocal group.

Jana and Dennis finally wound up in Branson, Missouri after stints in Naples and Tunisia, where she was program director at this lavish casino Dennis built. A rather unique situation, I'd say! She became the lead vocalist with Les Brown and His Band of Renown in Branson. She was also very pleasant to look at, and we were really good singing together.

Brenda Lee hired Jana and myself in 1992 to accompany her to Montreux, Switzerland where she was to perform on the Montreux Jazz Festival produced by Quincy Jones. Naturally, I included Jana on the "Kennedy Center Honors the Arts" shows in 1996 and 1998 in Washington DC.

Jana and I sang together on so many projects. "Too Cold at Home" and "Brother Jukebox" for Mark Chesnutt, the "Classic Love Songs" triple CD with Kenny Rogers, projects with Glen Campbell, BJ Thomas, Willie Nelson, Ronnie Milsap and many more. On the pre-recorded national anthem with Garth Brooks for the Super Bowl in January 1993, that's Jana hitting the high E on the last note. (Yeah, the HIGH E.)

Me, Quincy Jones and Jana King in Montreux, Switzerland doing the Montreux Jazz Festival with Brenda Lee that Quincy produced.

129

Kira Small

Lisa Silver called me one day in 2005 to hire me to sing background with her and another gal I'd never heard of. Lisa knew me so well and knew I didn't like experimenting with new singers on someone else's dime, so she quickly told me not to worry, that I would love this gal. Her name was Kira Small, and Lisa was correct, I loved her. She could read, she could fake it, she could write the charts herself, she played killer piano … she could do it all. Well, I've been working with her ever since, even as recently as two weeks ago. If I'm given a choice, I always hire Kira. She makes me look good!

When Jim Medlin (Martina McBride's band leader) called me in the summer of 2012 to hire me to put together a quartet to sing with Martina on her "Joy of Christmas" tour that year, of course I hired Kira. I also hired Marabeth Quin and Jon Mark Ivey, two more of my favorite singers. We did that tour through 2019 but were then shut down by COVID.

A little story about Kira: After doing that first session with Lisa and

Kira, we all went our separate ways.. I had a dinner date that night with a little cutie named Mikhel and was going for broke. I took her to the Wild Boar, an expensive restaurant, but hey, a man's gotta do what a man's gotta do. Anyway, we get there and are seated in this small private spot, and as we're conversing I can't help but be distracted by this really cool music coming from the lounge. The piano playing all the right chords, a beautiful voice, all that stuff. Finally, I asked the little cutie to excuse me. I just had to see who was in the lounge. I peek into the lounge and guess who it is? It's Kira.

I might've gotten lucky that night, but I can't remember. I do remember, though, that the lounge music was fantastic.

Kira Small and Marabeth Quin somewhere in the frigid North on the Martina "Joy of Christmas Tour".

130

Marabeth Quin

I became aware of Marabeth in the late '70s or early '80s when she was in a trio with Marty McCall and Bonnie Keen called First Call that worked mainly Christian contemporary recordings. As I've said earlier, I'm a softie for singers who can do it all, and she was also very pleasant to look at.

She was one of the select singers I used on The Bergen White Christmas Singers. I worked with her on so many projects, including Garth, Martina, Kenny Rogers, Willie Nelson, and Wynonna.

She was the alto in the marvelous quartet with me, Kira Small, and Mark Ivey on the equally marvelous "Joy of Christmas" tour with Martina McBride from 2012 through 2019. Anyone who knows me well knows that I am like Roy Orbison on stage, I hardly move at all. So naturally I hire good looking singers who have zero inhibitions, and are always moving with the beat. It's sort of like Gladys Knight's "Pips" dancing around a statue. Anyway, with Marabeth, Kira and Mark singing their parts and providing the choreography, we were pretty damn good, I tell ya!

131

Mark Ivey

Mark is without a doubt the best tenor I ever worked with. Jana King introduced me to Mark back when they were both part of the background quartet on "Nashville Now" with Ralph Emery. He's a singer who can fake it and read like crazy. Any and every opportunity that came my way, I hired Mark. Naturally, he was part of The Bergen White Christmas Singers.

We worked together for Kenny Rogers, Garth, Glen Campbell, Chris Isaak, Martina, Wynonna, Kathie Lee Gifford, Brenda Lee, and most recently on Martina McBride's "Joy of Christmas" tour. Mark and Kira Small led the dancing in the aisles of the tour bus in the middle of the night when we were on our way to the next stop. You really get to know someone when you're on tour with them. If you don't get along, it will only get worse on a bus. I've said many times before that I like to hire great musicians and singers because it makes me look good. That's the reason I always hired Mark.

Me, Kira Small and Mark Ivey at a mansion in East Nashville for a Martina Christmas video. Marabeth was conspicuously absent.

132

Wendy Suits

Me with Jennifer O'Brian and Wendy at the Cannery in the mid '70s.

Wendy came to Nashville from Memphis where she had been working with a "jingle mill" (doing commercials); she sang and wrote a lot of the spots. She was a great singer with a wide range; could sing soprano or alto, and she could read like crazy, so I loved working with her. She became a member of The Nashville Edition when Ricky Page moved to LA and could be seen weekly on the TV hit series "Hee Haw".

She was also extremely funny. You never knew what to expect from Wendy. There was never a dress code for the musicians and singers for sessions. Some would wear suits while some would be in overalls, or less. One day on a big session at RCA all the musicians and singers were gathering when Wendy struts in with this short, tight skirt and black, high-heeled boots that came up just over her knees. She walks right up to the singers booth and says, "These are my 'fuck me' boots." We all tried to think of something clever to say, but how do you follow that?

I was working a session one day with Wendy, Lisa Silver, and Buzz Cason at Eleven-Eleven Sound with Chips Moman producing. Both Wendy and Lisa are perfectionists so as we were recording, we'd sing a line and either Wendy or Lisa would stop us and say, "Oops, I can do that better." Mind you, it wasn't the producer stopping us, it was Wendy or Lisa wanting to make it perfect. Well, this went on and on for quite a while until finally I reached up and wrote "STFU" at the top of the chart. Both of the gals looked puzzled and whispered, "What does that mean?" I whispered back, "Shut the fuck up!"

133

Ricky Page

When I first got into the business in 1964 it seemed Ricky was everywhere. She was the soprano in The Nashville Edition with Hurshel Wiginton, Delores Edgin and Joe Babcock, and they were one of the hottest background groups in town. They split the session work three ways with The Jordanaires and The Anita Kerr Singers.

She was also singing about ninety percent of all the female lead vocals on the "sound-a-likes" I've mentioned before. She was covering Petula Clark, Dusty Springfield, Lesley Gore and many more through the '70s to early '80s until she moved to LA with her husband George Matola. Wendy Suits took her place with the group. Ricky could sing anything, sing any style, could read or fake it, which a singer is pretty much required to do in Nashville. I loved working with Ricky Page and did anytime I got the chance.

134

Tania Hancheroff

Blake Chancey hired me to sing background for a session about ten years ago, and when I asked who I would be singing with, he said Tania Hancheroff. I replied, "Never heard of her." His response: "Uncle Berg, you'll love her!" He was correct! She is absolutely as good as it gets. She was so good, she was Peter Cetera's (Chicago) background singer for his live concerts until he retired from touring in 2018.

Tania, Cindy Walker, and I survived the sixty-two-song marathon sessions on John Schneider of "Dukes of Hazard" fame. It was almost like being in a submarine with no way out. Had it not been for Tania and Cindy, I might not have been able to maintain my marvelous disposition, particularly after I discovered we did not get label credit. Everyone else did, but not the singers. (Kindly imagine some highly offensive profanity right here, if you will.)

I worked with Tania on sessions for Garth, Kenny Rogers, and Michael Feinstein, among many others.

The Singers: Tania Hancheroff

From left: Lisa Silver, Tania Hancheroff and Kira Small doing backgrounds for Michael Feinstein with Kyle Lehning producing.

135

Dennis Wilson

D ennis (not to be confused with Dennis Wilson of the Beach Boys) is a tall, quiet, marvelous singer who has this understated, wry sense of humor. When I was looking for other voices for the Chipmunks, I knew Dennis would be perfect as Simon. We survived the Chipmunks Christmas fiasco I told you about earlier, and came out on the other side with only hurt egos.

He was with me in Washington DC, for the Kennedy Center Honors when we did the music for the Roy Acuff and the Johnny Cash segments. He was also one of the background voices on most of the Brooks and Dunn hits. He was one of the select singers I hired for "The Bergen White Christmas Singers" project. Dennis, John Wesley Ryles, and I sang the only recorded version of "A Hacker's Lament" (a little known sorrowful tale about a golfer's bad day). I worked with Dennis on so many recordings, including Kenny Rogers, Brenda Lee, Kathie Lee Gifford, Glen Campbell, and Wynonna, to mention just a few.

136

The Hollidays

The Hollidays, Mary and Ginger, were hot in the late '60s and through the '70s. They had a third gal who sang with them a lot named Temple Rizor. With Jeannie Green they sang on a lot of Elvis' stuff like "Suspicious Minds", "In the Ghetto", "Kentucky Rain", and also worked on some of his live shows. They also worked with Jerry Reed on "When You're Hot You're Hot" and "Amos Moses", and with Billy Swan on "I Can Help".

I worked with Ginger on so many jingles produced by Ron Chancey. Ron worked with Jack Smith from the Leo Burnette Company in Chicago, so Ginger gave in and married Jack since she was with him so much already. I think that marriage lasted until the session was over. Sounds like one of my marriages.

There's a photo on the screen in the lounge at Ray Stevens's CabaRay that shows Buzz Cason, Carol Montgomery, Mary Holliday, and me. It says we were doing background vocals for Bob Dylan at Columbia Studios. Funny, neither Buzz nor I ever remember working with Bob Dylan. Seems like we would remember that! Maybe Mary remembers. If I ever see her again, I'll ask.

137

Cindy Walker

Ron Chancey used to bring Cindy and Ava Aldridge up from Muscle Shoals when he wanted a soulful sound. He would mix Buzz Cason and me with them, hoping they would make us sound soulful as well. Buzz and I used to call it our "riverboat" sound. I have absolutely no idea what that meant, but we said it a lot, and with great conviction.

Cindy has this gorgeous, pure soprano voice that can blend with any group of singers, whether they're worth a damn or not. She has a way of making everyone sound better than they are. I've worked with Cindy ever since Ron first introduced us. Cindy, Tania Hancheroff, and I worked recently with John Schneider on a marathon sixty-two-song project. We survived, and are still speaking to each other.

The beginning of the end ... and other stuff, if you're still reading this.

138

The Copyists

George Tidwell, who was my first copyist, introduced me to Joe Layne when George got too busy doing his own work. Joe is Italian, a great cook, and always called me "Babes". He was an excellent jazz pianist and played piano on the "Morning Show with Teddy Bart", if anyone remembers that. Joe was a great copyist, and this was back when copyists copied by hand.

Copyists, like arrangers, were on call twenty-four hours a day trying to satisfy the whims of the producers, many of whom would wait until the last minute to decide they wanted strings or horns. So I would call Joe, needing to have charts ready at 10 a.m. the next day, and here we would go. I would be up in my third-floor office writing charts in the middle of the night while Joe slept with his head on the dining room table until I dropped a chart down to the first floor, then Joe would wake up and start copying. We operated like this for twenty-five years until Joe quit in the early '90s.

After Joe quit, I switched over to Tom McAninch, who copied on the computer. The charts looked like sheet music; they were just beautiful. After Tom, I teamed up with Eberhard Ramm, the best French horn player I'd ever heard. To this day I'm still working with "Ebschtick" who advised me right away that I was writing all the symphony charts in the wrong form. I thought, "Why the hell hasn't someone told me this before?" I guess it's never too late to learn.

Anyway, copyists are valuable for so many reasons. When something goes wrong on a session, the arranger can always blame the copyist, since they are never there to defend themselves. Seriously, though, I couldn't have survived without my copyists.

139

The CMA Awards

David Briggs and I were co-music directors for the CMA Awards starting in 1988. Until that time, Bill Walker was the music director and he always had an orchestra, rhythm section, string section, brass, woodwinds, the whole works. The execs at CMA decided they wanted the music to sound more country, so for instance, if George Jones was coming on stage, instead of the music sounding like the score from "The High and the Mighty" there would be guitars, dobros, etc. Also, they wanted the music to be pre-recorded, which was a big change. That worked great in a lot of instances, but sucked in others.

The first year David and I did the show, all the preparation and rehearsals were done and it was showtime! I was a little rusty at live TV and was just trying to stay out of the way, so I decided I would watch director Walter C. Miller do his thing from the control room. The ever-increasing tension was palpable as I slipped in the back door, and wow, it was impressive! Walter sitting in the middle of the front row with maybe twenty TV monitors in front of him. Pam Repp to his left. Ally Gifford to his right. John Fields next to Ally, with Christine Clark Bradley just behind. Jan Ray next to Pam, then Sharon "Boom Boom" Taylor. Must've been ten on that front row, the sound guy in the next row, then a hive of television executives hovering. Behind them all was this pleasant fellow from New York named Bill, the lighting guy. All these people had very specific functions, with Walter seemingly controlling everything. It was an amazing thing to watch!

I'm really diggin' on this controlled chaos, but in an effort again to stay out of the way, I crept over against this wall and inadvertently leaned against the switch that turns off the power to the lighting guy. So Walter is shouting, "Camera one, zoom in", "More sound", "Lights stage right." Nothing. So Walter shouts again, "Lights, stage right." Still nothing, so Walt screams, "What the fuck is going on? Where's the fuckin' lights?" Bill screams back, "I sitting in the fuckin' dark and can't see a damn thing!"

It was as if a massive leak had just been discovered in a submarine. Absolute bedlam! Everyone was scrambling around until finally someone found the switch exactly where I had been standing and flipped the power back on. Probably took only about three seconds, but it seemed like a lifetime. Needless to say, I got out of the control room! I reminded Walter of it years later, and he called me an asshole.

One instance where the pre-recording aspect sucked was with Ricky Van Shelton. I can't remember the year, but Ricky was up for some big awards, and David and I were pre-recording his song. We had the finest musicians you could get. Ricky's producer Steve Buckingham was there with us, and Ricky was on the road somewhere. We cut the track to Steve's satisfaction, he called Ricky, we played it for him, and he loved it. No problem.

So we're at the rehearsals and it's Ricky's time to rehearse, but when the track starts playing, he stops it immediately, complaining it's too fast or too slow and that he's not going to sing to that track even though both he and Steve had approved it. As always, it's the CMA's fault. So David and I go back to the studio to adjust the track to satisfy his complaints. We get back to the Opry House and David takes the new adjusted track to Ricky's bus, but Ricky won't even listen to it. At this point, Irving Waugh, this British gentleman who was one of the upper execs at CMA for years, has had enough of this shit so he instructs security to "kick his arse" (*arse* is British for ass) off the property. Finally Ricky comes to his senses and agrees to do the show—but that episode either led to Irving Waugh's quitting the show, or being fired from the show. The fault was totally Ricky Van Shelton's, but the CMA was blamed for being unreasonable.

Another grisly episode: Again, I can't remember the year, but George Jones had come back strong after a lengthy absence and had a big hit on a song called "Choices" produced by Keith Stegall. The problem: George was nominated in a category called the Horizon Award, which was basically for new acts. Well, George was *not* a new act. Also in this category was an act called Lonestar, whose record was so big it had crossed over into the pop market. Due to time constraints, all four of the acts in this particular category were required to cut their songs to a minute and a half. No one complained except George, who said he would not cut his song down at all. I seem to recall it was at least three and a half minutes long. George simply was not going to cut his song and threatened not to do the show at all unless he could do his entire song. The CMA stood their ground. Why should he be allowed to do his entire song when all the rest had to cut them to a minute and a half? So George didn't do the show.

The night of the show, for some reason, I'm standing at one of the back entrances to the Opry House when Keith Stegall comes in wearing his tux, walks up to me all smiles, shakes my hand, and says, "Have a great show." I know this might not sound weird, but Keith Stegall had never spoken to me at all before that. I'm not sure he has since. I should've known something was up. You see, Keith also produced Alan Jackson, who was up for Entertainer of the Year and Record of the Year. The tune Alan was doing was "Pop a Top". So Alan is performing, does about a minute and a half of "Pop a Top", then switches to "Choices". The crowd goes crazy, since everyone thought the CMA had treated George Jones so poorly. Here was another instance of the CMA getting the blame. But what would you have done? No matter what you do, you're wrong.

Most acts were very easy to work with, but some were a complete pain in the ass. Maybe an act like Rascal Flatts wasn't difficult themselves, but their management was so hard to get any information from that it gave the act a bad image. It was the same thing with Alan Jackson. When we did the CMAs in New York we didn't know what song he was doing until the dress rehearsal. And then at the rehearsal, he did a different song than he actually did on the show! Absurd! How do you possibly prepare for that kind of shit? But hey, he was Alan Jackson, so he could get away with it.

Garth Brooks, Vince Gill, Kenny Rogers, and Brad Paisley were an absolute delight to work with. They would actually communicate with us themselves instead of having someone else speak for them. What a concept! Acts like Hank Williams, Jr., KD Lang, and Ricky Van Shelton simply could not have been any more difficult.

The "Dixie Bitches" were the worst! Sometimes an act can get so big they manage to get their heads squirmed so far up their own asses, they suffer brain damage. The CMA bent over backwards to accommodate everything they asked for, and in retrospect, I think a real firm "No fuckin' way" would've been the proper response.

When Taylor Swift first came on the show, she was so thrilled to be there she would do anything she was asked to do. Each year after that, she got bigger and bigger and more and more difficult to work with.

On a lighter note, one year I was rehearsing on stage with an act, and when we finished I was walking back to the production office when this guy with a lot of cameras stopped me and said, "Oh, sir, could you possibly give me just a few minutes for a short interview? I won't take much of your time, I know how busy you are." I'm thinking, "Why the hell does this guy want to interview me?" But then I thought, "Well, how cool is this? This guy wants to interview people in the background, not necessarily the stars, but also the folks doing the grunt work." So while he's setting up the lights and the camera I'm thinking, "How cool is this man? This is cooler than cool." When he's set up he says, "Are you ready, sir?" I nod, then he turns on the camera and says, "So, David, tell me about your new single." I interrupt him and ask, "Who's David?" He thought I was David Frizzell. So much for the "cool" aspect.

140

The CMA Music Festival

The CMA used to have this music fest out at Opryland where they had all kinds of seminars, performances, etc. For this one particular seminar, there were about ten music people representing pretty much every facet of the business. I can't remember who was the moderator, but the panel had Kyle Lehning and Tony Brown representing producers, Harlan Howard and Jack Clement for writers, Jerry House was there for the radio people, Larrie Londin, Shane Keister, and David Briggs were there for musicians, and I was there for arrangers. Briggs and I were sitting next to each other at this long table, each of the panelists had their own microphone, yada, yada, yada.

The room was packed with DJs, promotional experts, and touring experts. The moderator would recognize someone in the audience to ask a question and then decide which panelist could best answer the question. After about an hour of this, someone asked a question that the moderator thought I would be the most qualified to answer. I straightened up in my chair and leaned toward my mic, and just as the spotlight hit me, David poured a full cup of hot coffee into my lap. On purpose! I'm fidgeting all over the place trying to regain my composure while trying to keep the coffee from running into my cool cowboy boots. Thankfully, the moderator decided to let someone else answer that particular question. That's what I get for sitting next to Briggs.

141

The Nashville Strings

Ever since 1965, the strings had a "system" going on. I was too stupid to know it at the time, but Brenton Banks would hire Lillian Hunt and Lillian would hire Brenton regardless of what the session might call for. I recall meeting Lillian, a known violinist, and a good one at that, at my very first string session where she showed up playing viola. I realize you're probably thinking, "What's the big deal?" The big deal was, and still is to this day, that contractors make deals with each other to use certain players, even though there are other players who are better. Both Brenton and Lillian were very kind and helpful to me in the beginning of my career, and what they were doing as contractors *then* happens to be the same thing most contractors are doing *today*. I cannot deny that some great records were cut back in the day when Brenton and Lillian were contracting, however, I was slowly becoming aware that what we were getting was not the absolute best.

From the very beginning of my career as an arranger, I was always asking the producers for larger string sections—I love the sound of the string sections in symphonies, which are usually forty to fifty players. I preferred to write the violins up above the staff (which means very high in their register), and in some instances, I would have them *way* above the staff. Much of my influence about strings came from the pop music I listened to. For example, the Glen Campbell recordings, "Wichita Lineman" and "By the Time I Get to Phoenix", Gordon Lightfoot's "If You Could Read My Mind", and John Denver's "Annie" all had these high violins.

The problem is, when you've only got five or six violins (and they happen to not be the best violinists) it can become frightening to one's ears.

About this time, some of the players noticed my dismay and approached me about making a change. They suggested that they could bring in better players, to which I said, "From where?" They replied, "Right here in Nashville." I asked, "Well, why haven't I ever seen or heard them before?" One of these guys, Marvin Chantry, was one of the better viola players, and the other was a gifted violinist named Shelly Kurland. I ended up choosing Shelly because traditionally the leader/contractor is a violinist. Right off the bat, I told Shelly that if I was going to hire him, I wanted him to guarantee me the absolute best players he could get, because I knew some of the older players were going to be unhappy and we had to make it count.

The next session I did with Shelly happened to be on my conclusive album called "Finale". I was looking at a string section, that with a few exceptions, I hadn't seen before. It was then that I first met Carl Gorodetzky; second chair violin next to Shelly, as well as Roy Christianson and Martha McCrory who were on cello. They were absolutely marvelous!

As expected, the players who were suddenly not being called for any sessions were upset, and I received letters from three or four of them asking to get back in. Unfortunately, I couldn't ask Shelly to give me the best players he could get and then turn around and say, "But what about so and so, and so and so?"

Shelly was always trying to improve on the section with my total blessing. I think it was 1980 when he persuaded Conni Ellisor (straight from Juilliard) to move from Denver to Nashville. She was not only cute, but an excellent violinist.

Shelly always treated me as though I was his number one client. Each and every time I called him for a session, no matter how many simultaneous sessions he had going on, he was always there for me. I can say I had zero complaints with Shelly—you could even say I was ass deep in gratitude! In my usual ignorant state, I had no idea what was going on in the underbelly of the section.

One day Carl called me and asked if I'd meet with him, Marvin Chantry, George Binkley, and Roy Christianson at Marvin's house, but he told me not to mention it to anyone else. Sure … I'll meet with them ….

It was during that meeting that I was informed about the tension and unrest that had been going on. I was flabbergasted because I had been under the impression everything was "peachy". They asked if they could host a larger meeting, and if it could be at my house, to which I agreed. I later realized that this was an egregious lapse in judgement.

I believe that requested meeting took place in November of 1981, and there must've been sixteen to twenty people present. I'm talking producers and players, all of which were determined to oust Shelly from his leader/contractor status and move Carl into the vacant spot. Even though I had nothing at all to do with this decision, it appeared I did since the meeting took place at my home.

Shelly never forgave me for this, even though I feel I was totally innocent of everything except incredible stupidity. And then, even though the group had rid themselves of Shelly, there was still a tremendous amount of turmoil, so much so that two different string sections were created. Carl would head "The Nashville String Machine", and Conni brought in her own players called the "A-Strings". Both of these sections were adequate, but after a few years, I begged them to combine the best players from both sections to create one kickin' ass section. This finally became a reality, partly because Conni was pregnant at the time and was sick of dealing with all the horseshit. Carl remained the contractor and the name of our new kickin' ass section remained the same, "The Nashville String Machine".

Everything seemed to go smoothly for a while, and the string business was booming! As I mentioned earlier, I had spent my entire career trying to get larger string sections because I loved the sound. Obviously, the larger the section, the more expensive. At the same time, the American Federation of Musicians was consistently trying to increase our wages, which is exactly their job. To show you how effective they were, take for example, in my first year, 1965, I'd pick up a check for a session at the Union and it would be $56, now, it goes for close to $400! Pretty sweet —doncha know! However, musician pay rose, lots of recording budgets shrunk, so unfortunately, it ended up pretty much pricing big string sections out of the game, except for the really big artists, like George Strait or Garth Brooks.

There were a few players who acknowledged this trend and figured if they could get ahead of it by persuading producers that they didn't need to hire sixteen players, (if they could convince them to hire a string quartet and stack it over and over), then the producers only had to pay four players. I suppose you could say they were shrewd, but this thinking has not only greatly damaged the string business, but the entire music business as a whole. Unless you were lucky enough to be one of the string quartet, you are basically out of work. Those are the cold hard business facts, and it affected a lot of players negatively. That really sucks the big one if you ask me.

On the artistic side of things, if you stack a string quartet four times, it doesn't sound like sixteen players, instead, it sounds exactly like what it is – a string quartet stacked four times. This is not what a string quartet was intended for. "Chamber Music" is where it came from, and an arranger writes for a string quartet quite differently than he writes for a larger section… or at least he should. I realize it's a fine line between what a recording needs and what the label can afford, so as is usually the case, money wins over art.

About ten years ago Ross Copperman was producing Darius Rucker, wanting strings on this one song called "Another Night with You". He sent the track to me, and then we had a conversation about it. I asked how many strings I could use. He answered that he could only afford three players: two violins and one viola. I said, "No way am I gonna try to write what I'm hearing with only three players." He said he simply could not afford any more players. Since I had already pretty much written the chart in my head, I offered to write it free of charge, but I needed four more players, and they could be paid what he would've paid me for the arrangement. He didn't like the idea, but eventually relented and we cut it. I think it turned out much better as a result.

Through the years, I've worked with some marvelous contractors beginning with Brenton Banks and Lillian Hunt, Shelly Kurland, Carl Gorodetsky, Pam Sixfin and finally Conni Ellisor. These people, and the sections they hired, were my lifeline. From the mid 60's until the present, I've relied on string players and I absolutely love these people. Every one of them! I lovingly called them my "stringabillies". Producers hired me to write the string arrangements, I hired the string sections, and I'm telling the absolute truth when I say, that the strings in Nashville today are absolutely as good as you can get. Period!

142

The Nashville Number System

The Nashville number system has been written about and discussed so much, I hardly think I have anything new to offer, but ... as marvelous a tool as it is, particularly for rhythm players (piano, bass, guitars, etc.), it is sometimes impractical to use from an arranger's point of view. Over the years I've found that when I've written for a full session—rhythm, strings, horns, background voices, the whole works—when I pick up the charts at the end of the session, the rhythm players have scribbled numbers above my chord symbols, since that is what they are used to. It's totally understandable. I even got to the point I would write all the orchestra the proper way, but write numbers for the rhythm section. There are certain songs where the number system can get quite confusing, to the point that you tend to forget what number 1 is.

In an effort to try to explain simply what the number system is (for those who already know what it is, please bear with me for a moment) it's actually very simple. It doesn't matter what key you are in, the numbers work. For this illustration, let's say we're in the key of C. C would be 1,

C# would be 1#, D would be 2, etc., all the way up to C again. Let's take a really simple song like "Jingle Bells," and we want to do this in the key of C. With chord symbols it would go like this, in 2/4 time: C C C C F C D G C C C C F C G C. That's the chorus to the song. In numbers it would be: 1 1 1 1 4 1 2 5 1 1 1 1 4 1 5 1. Like I've said, changing the key wouldn't matter; the numbers would be the same. You've just got to remember what key you're in.

Some songs change chords so much, you think you've modulated to a different key when you haven't, or you have but don't realize it. When someone asks, "What key are we in?", someone answers, "Don't look at me, I'm lost!". On recordings where a male and female are doing a duet, most of the time you need to change keys at least once to accommodate the singers' ranges. Let's say the female starts in the key of C, but when it's the male's turn to sing, you've got to go to E flat. Do you call the E flat a 1 flat or a 3 flat ? Then after he sings a bit, you modulate and go back to the female, and all of a sudden the 1 is something else entirely.

As you can see, the number system can sometimes be very confusing. Number system purists would argue the point, because in country music the number system is perfect about ninety percent of the time. However, sometimes old-fashioned chord symbols are the safest way to go for more complex songs.

The following are three songs with chord symbols first, then the same song with the number system. The first is "He Stopped Loving Her Today" written by Bobby Braddock and Curly Putnam, recorded by George Jones, produced by Billy Sherrill. It is absolutely brilliant in its simplicity. Three chords all the way through, except for one modulating chord. Next would be "The Christmas Song" written by Mel Tormé and recorded by everyone who ever recorded a Christmas album. And third would be "After the Love Is Gone" written by David Foster, Jay Graydon, and Bill Champlin, recorded by Earth, Wind and Fire. As you will see on "The Christmas Song" and "After the Love Is Gone", the numbers begin to look like Greek hieroglyphics, ancient inscriptions, if you will.

After seeing these three songs with both approaches, you can see which approach is the most efficient. It's pretty clear to me, but you can make up your own mind. Good luck with the numbers on the last two songs.

The Nashville Number System

Right Place at the Write Time

The Nashville Number System

"THE CHRISTMAS SONG"

♩=62

C G F Em Dm Em7 Eb9 Dm9 Db9(add11) **(A)** VERSE C Dm7 Em7 F6

C Gm7 C9#5 F9 Bb6/9 C/E F6 C/G F#m7(add11) B7

E△ Fm7 Bb9 Eb△ Dm9 G9 **(B)** VERSE C Dm7 Em7 F△9 C Gm7 C9#5

F△9 Bb6/9 C/G Dm/G Em/G F#m7(add11) B9 Em7 Am7 Dm7 G(b9)

C **(C)** BRIDGE Gm7 C7 Gm7 C(b9) F△9 F6 Fm7 Bb7

Eb△ C♭7 Am7 D9 Dm7/G G9 Db9 **(D)** RELEASE C Dm7 Em7 F△9

Am7 Bb△ Gm7 C7#5 F△9 Bb6/9 C/G Dm/G Em/G F#m7 B-9

Em7 F△9   Em7 Am7 Dm7 G(b9) C G F Em Dm
                                           MERRY
CHRISTMAS   MERRY CHRISTMAS   NORTH TO FROM   TO   YOU

Em7 Eb9 Dm7 Db7(add11) C6/9

301

Right Place at the Write Time

"THE CHRISTMAS SONG"

The Nashville Number System

Right Place at the Write Time

The Nashville Number System

Right Place at the Write Time

(handwritten chord chart with Nashville number notation)

143

Arranging 101

So many times I've been asked by aspiring arrangers how I got started. To be honest I'm actually embarrassed to try to answer the question. Inadvertently I suppose, I learned so much simply because of my upbringing but never did I study music theory or orchestration and all that because I was not going to be in the music business. Instead, I was planning to play baseball. I stumbled into the business doing sound-a-likes for a company that was copying "hit" records, and finally was asked to arrange them. I was being paid a retainer to "copy" hit records. Unfortunately that course is not offered at Julliard.

I believe great vocalists are born with the talent to sing, just as I believe great athletes are born with great athletic abilities. Just because a person wants with all their heart and soul to be a great recording artist or athlete doesn't mean they can be. No matter how much they study, if they weren't born with it, it's simply not gonna happen. I remember hearing a famous singer say she would advise aspiring singers to never, ever give up. "If you want it badly enough and keep trying, you will have it!" she said. What a crock of shit! It doesn't matter if you have degrees from Juilliard, Berkeley School of Music, or anywhere else; if you weren't born with the ability to arrange, it's simply not gonna happen.

I'm not saying that studying music isn't important. As a matter of fact, I'm saying the opposite: learn everything you possibly can because it will surely be a benefit to you somewhere along the way if you actually wind up arranging. Let's say for a moment that you were not born with these talents but you've studied at all the universities and gotten all the degrees and finally someone asks you to arrange for them. You'll know technically all that you need to know but where do the ideas come from? Do you steal them from other arrangements you've heard? Believe me, a lot of arrangers (myself included) do that if they can't come up with something of their own. Also the plain truth is, it's impossible to come up with something that is entirely original, never been done before. So back to my question: where do the ideas come from?

When I'm given a CD or an MP3 with tracks I'm asked to add orchestration to, I will listen to each tune over and over (if time permits). Years ago I'd be given a cassette or reel-to-reel tape with four songs on it and they wanted to record the strings the next day so I didn't have time to listen to them much and had to just start writing. Back in the '70s and '80s, that was the rule, not the exception. I was forced to write under those circumstances so often it became a problem for me if I was given a week to write the charts. I would write them and rewrite them over and over. Too much time!

I always loved it when I was asked to arrange for a full session: rhythm, strings, horns, background voices all at once. Live! If given the time I would drive around in my car listening to the songs, getting ideas that I would scribble down on some little bitty score paper I had in my car. Finally I would sit down at my keyboard and experiment with different chord changes and then finally I would start putting it on the score. It's such a treat to hear the arrangement come alive in the studio. Sometimes when you're under the most pressure is when it all kicks in and you write your best. The chart I wrote on the flight to London for Michael Card's "God Will Provide a Lamb" was a prime example of that, but without that innate ability I couldn't have done it.

Sometimes you can sit at your desk for a while struggling to come up with something, and instead you come up with nothing so you quit writing, get on your John Deere, start cutting the grass, and then all of a sudden these ideas just come from everywhere. Again, I scribble them down on my little bitty score paper and go back to work. Something has got to inspire you to get you going. Sometimes it's a drive in the car. Sometimes it's the John Deere. Sometimes it's sex. Many a chart has been inspired by a little roll in the hay, something that releases your mind and lets you start over.

If your ambition is to become a successful arranger, you've got to learn how to write something that pleases you but more importantly pleases the producer. You can write what you think is the most incredible chart that's ever been written, but if the producer doesn't like it, it sucks. Plain and simple! When you are beginning in your career, you are trying to figure out what the producers want, yet still be creative in order to add your own "thing" to it. It's a very fine line. I learned quickly that Tom Collins (who produced Ronnie Milsap, Barbara Mandrell, and Sylvia) loved glissandos. If I didn't include them in my chart he would ask me to add it at the session. Yet there are other producers who hate them. For instance John Farrar, an LA producer, hired me to arrange the strings for Olivia Newton John's album called "Don't Stop Believing". The first thing he said to me was he hated glissandos. I left them out of her charts.

Many producers wanted to hear strings on their records simply because it was "happening" at that time (the mid '70s to the mid '90s), but they didn't want the strings to get in the way, meaning they didn't want them to take attention away from the artist. Some producers knew exactly what they wanted the strings to do; others didn't have a clue. Billy Sherrill knew to the point where he would hum licks to you that he wanted to hear.

On one particular session Billy told me exactly what he wanted on a song that he said was going to be the single. He said I could write whatever I wanted on the other songs, they didn't matter. We did the "important" song first and he loved it. Then he went to his office while I added strings to the songs that didn't matter. When Billy heard what I had done on one of the other songs he said, "Dammit, you asshole, you've made me change my mind about what the single is."

Producers are a peculiar sort to say the least. The fine line I mentioned before is being able to add your own creativity to a record but never forgetting that your opinion doesn't mean shit; it's got to please the producer. Even if you think it's perfect, you've got to always be prepared to change your chart, to suit whatever the producer wants to hear, even if you think their idea sucks. The following are some computer scores that I arranged over the years.

Arranging 101

Nightlife

Score — Willie Nelson
arranged by Bergen White

Shuffle (what else?) ♩=70

Right Place at the Write Time

Nightlife - p. 2 - Score

Arranging 101

Nightlife - p. 3 - Score

Right Place at the Write Time

Arranging 101

Score — For The Good Times
Willie Nelson
arranged by Bergen White

Right Place at the Write Time

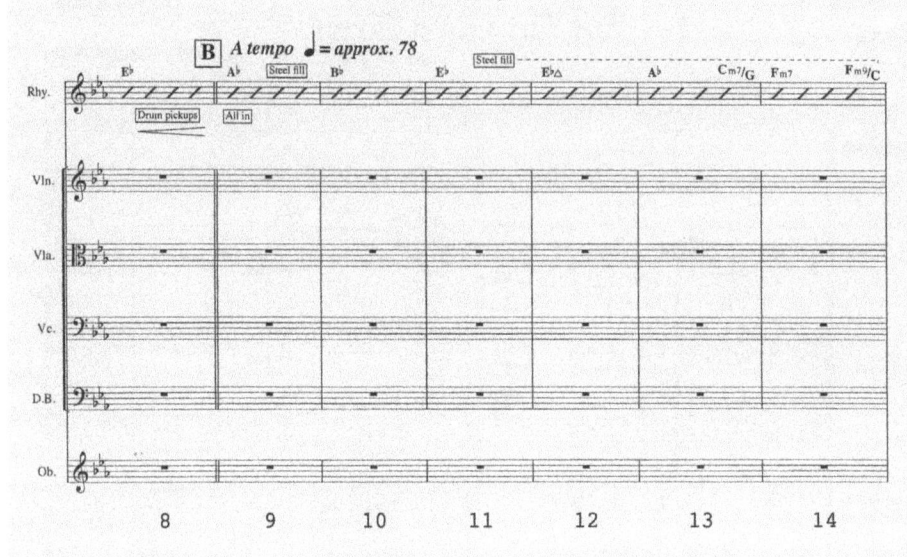

Arranging 101

For The Good Times - p. 3 - Score

Right Place at the Write Time

For The Good Times - p. 4 - Score

Arranging 101

For The Good Times - p. 5 - Score

Right Place at the Write Time

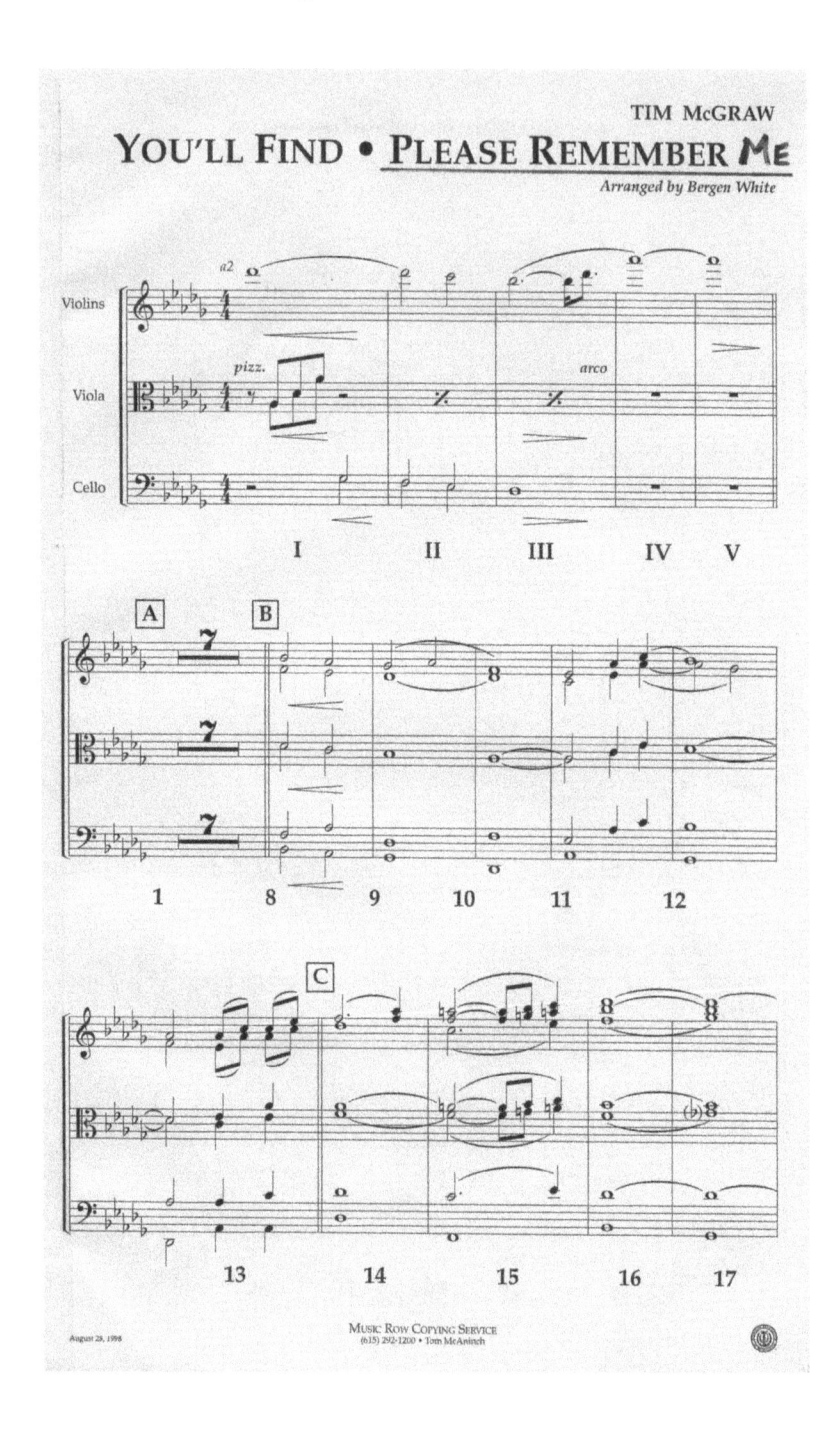

You'll Find Better Love • Please Remember Me

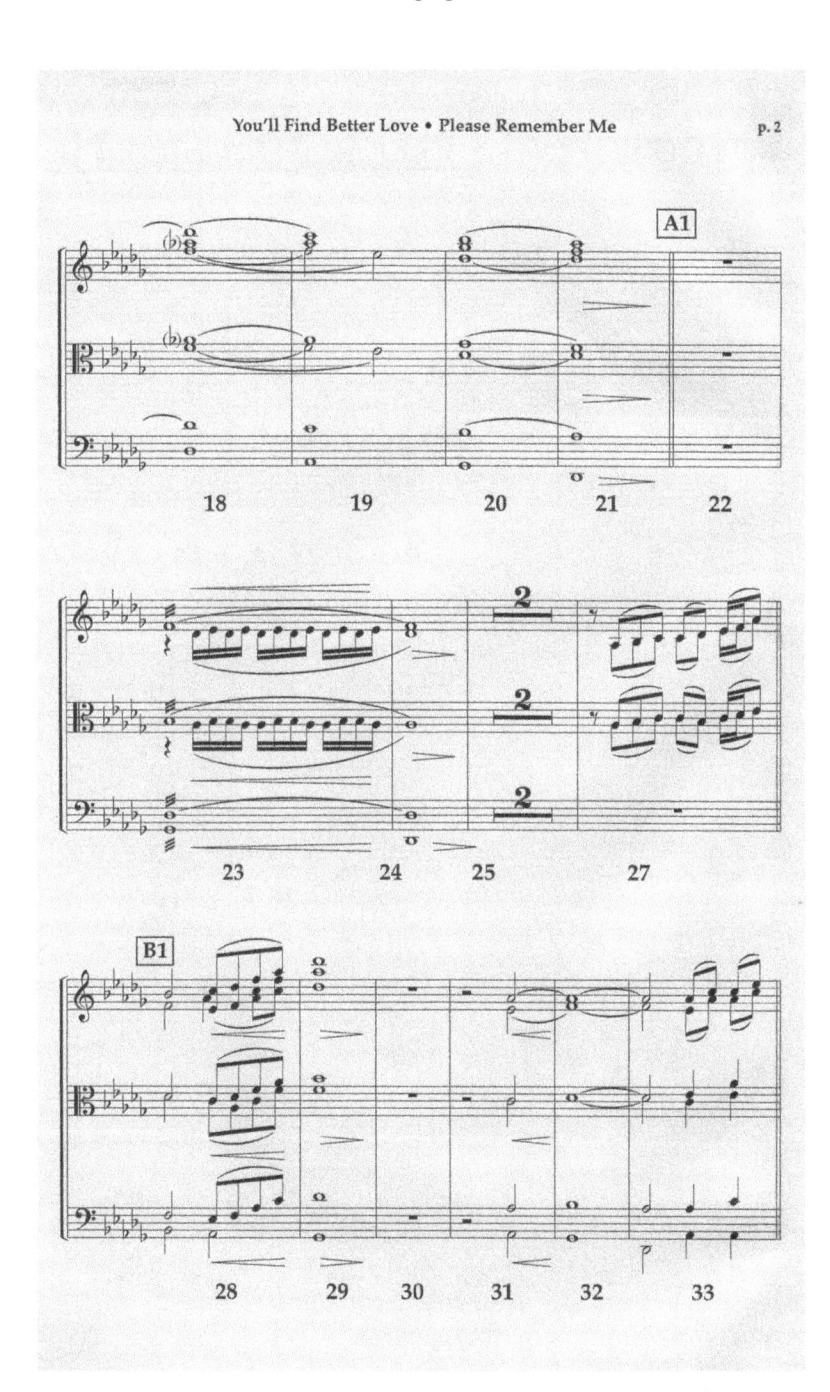

Right Place at the Write Time

You'll Find Better Love • Please Remember Me

You'll Find Better Love • Please Remember Me

You'll Find Better Love • Please Remember Me p. 5

VINCE GILL
IF YOU EVER HAVE FOREVER IN MIND
Arranged by Bergen White
Shuffle ♩=62
Acoustic Gtr. (shuffle)
F
Dm7
Gm7
C9
brushes
kick
drums: simile throughout
bass
Rhythm
Piano
Violins
BGVs
a2
Ooh
I
II
A
piano fills
F7
B♭
1
2
3
4
C7
5
6
7
Music Row Copying Service
(615) 292-1200 • Tom McAninch
February 1999

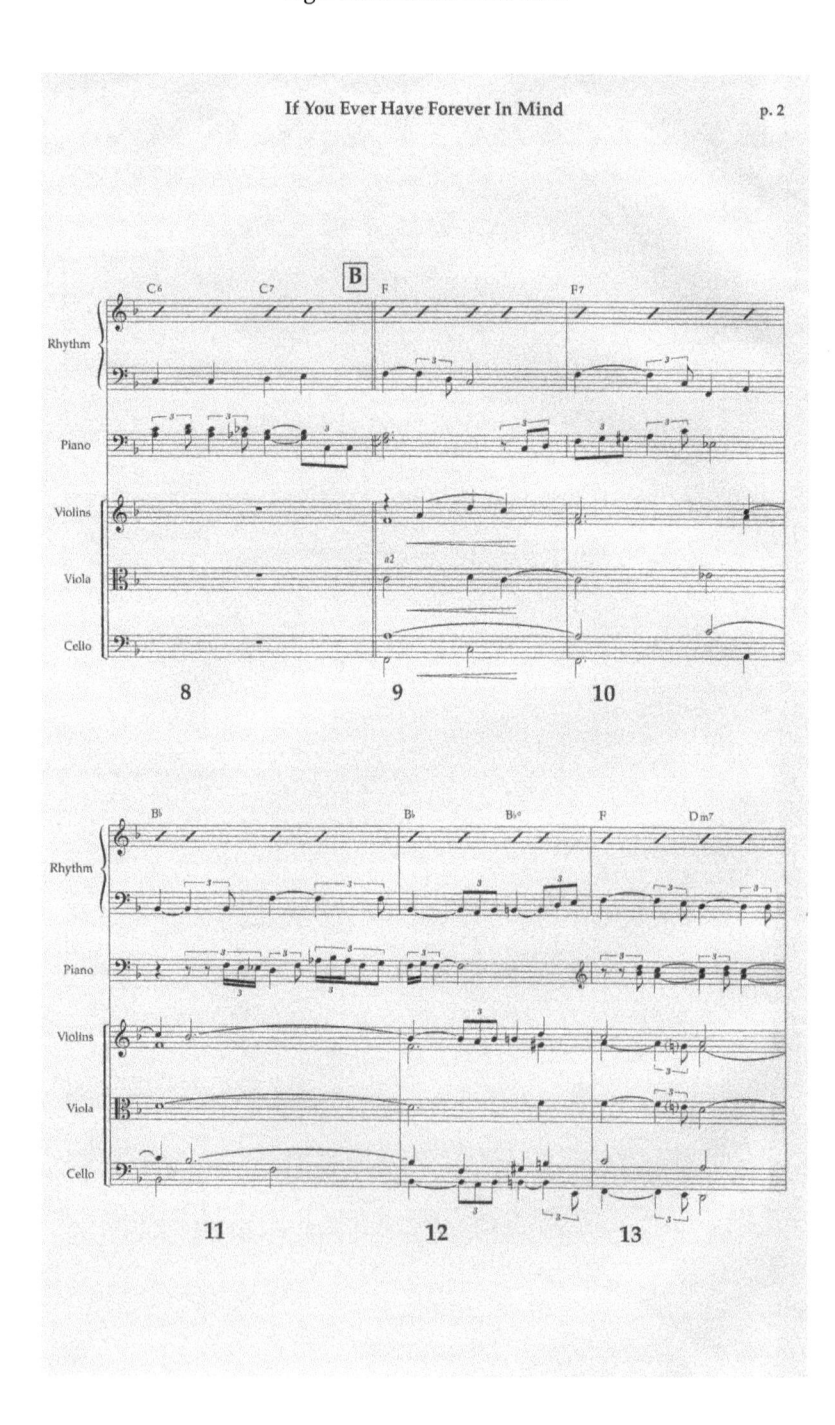

If You Ever Have Forever In Mind

If You Ever Have Forever In Mind

Right Place at the Write Time

If You Ever Have Forever In Mind

p. 4

Arranging 101

If You Ever Have Forever In Mind

p. 5

Right Place at the Write Time

If You Ever Have Forever In Mind

Arranging 101

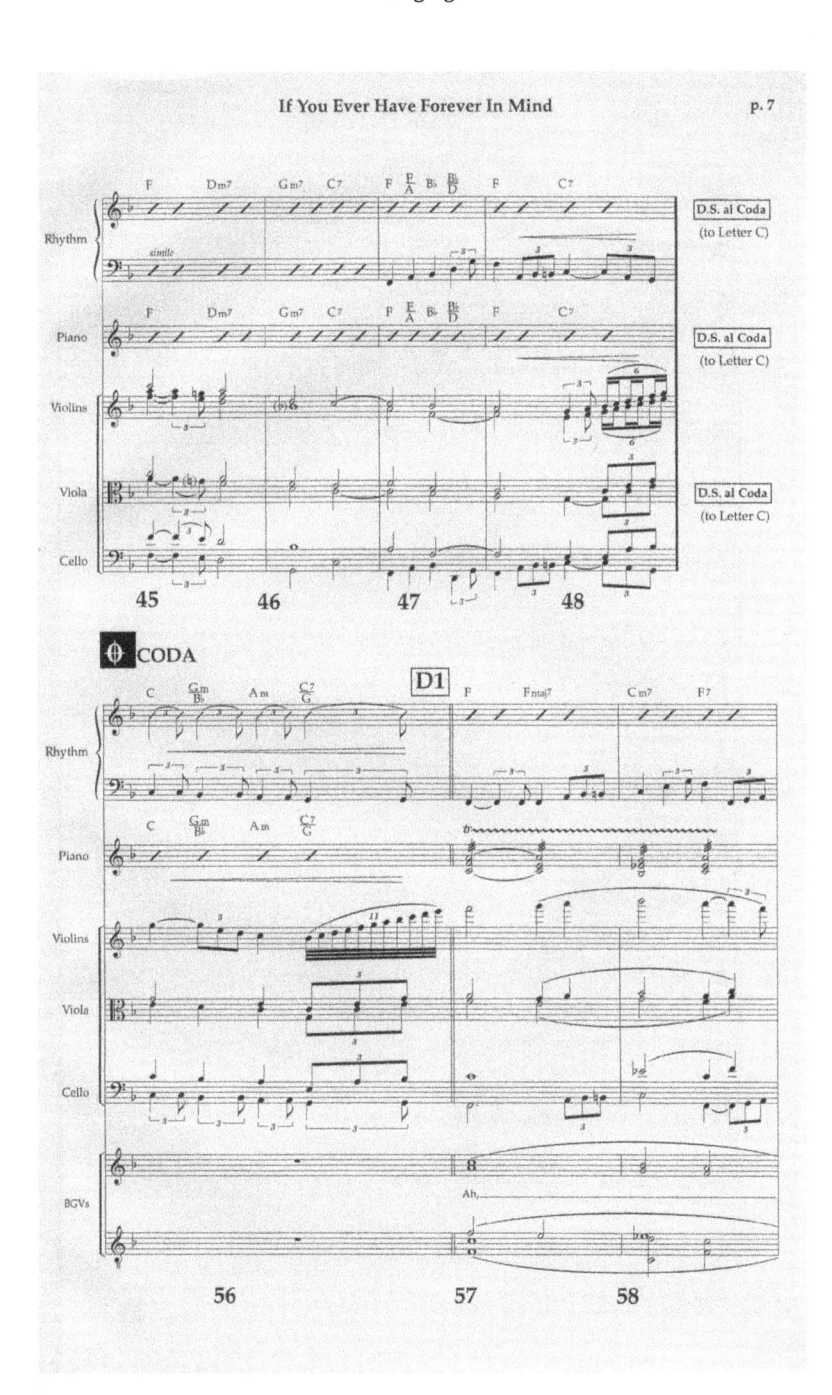

If You Ever Have Forever In Mind

p. 7

Right Place at the Write Time

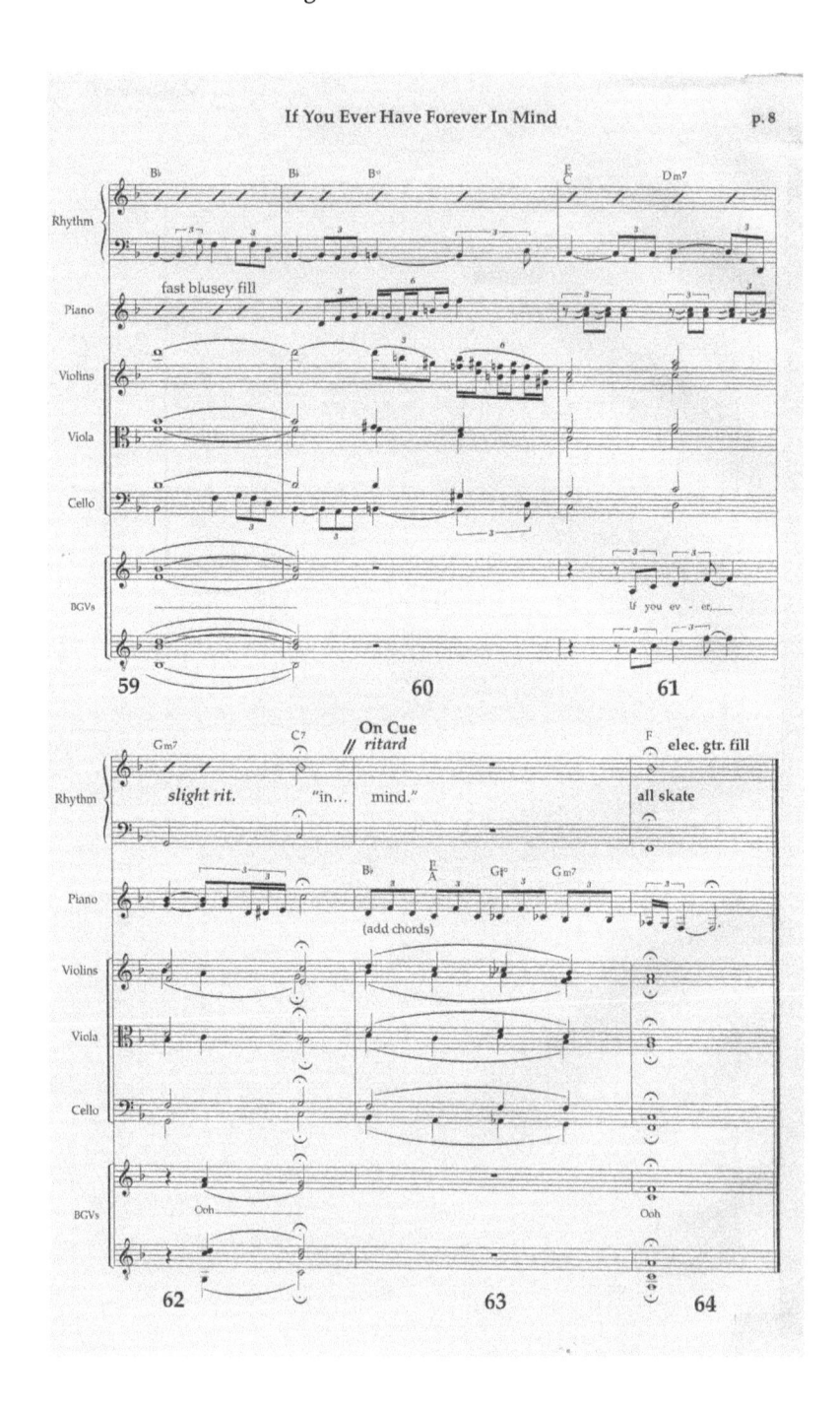

144

For Women Only

In 1967, Wayne Moss and I started recording an album, with me as the artist. We had no particular goal in mind, but we recorded anyway because that's what people do in this business ... they record stuff. We did that for about two years, and then one day we scheduled an appointment with Larry Butler, who at the time was head of A&R at Capitol Records, Nashville. We pitched "Second Lover's Song" and just happened to put "Hurt So Bad" on the tape also.

When we met with Larry, a couple guys from the LA office of Capitol were with him. One of them was named Karl Engemann. After we played the songs for them, this Engemann fellow got real excited about "Hurt So Bad" and suggested he take the tape to LA to try to get us a deal there since these cuts were pop, not country. We were excited as well until about two months later, when the number one record in the country was "Hurt So Bad" by the Letterman. Karl Engemann's brother was Bob Engemann of the Letterman. Everyone was telling us they copied our cut. They copied us after we copied Little Anthony and the Imperials.

The lesson here is you need to be careful whom you play your shit for! Not only did we not get the deal with Capitol, but they also stole our idea ... that we had stolen from Little Anthony. Thieves stealing from thieves! Ha-ha! Serves them right. Wait ... serves us right too! I guess.

Shortly after that, Bob Beckham introduced me to Shelby Singleton. Bob was encouraging Shelby to sign me to a recording contract and sign me he did, but he wanted Wayne and me to finish the album in a hurry for release. So we started feverishly looking for suitable songs to cut to add to the eight or so we had already finished. We found two songs by Barry Mann and Cynthia Weil, "She Is Today" and "Lisa Was", and two songs by David Gates, "Look at Me" and "Gone Again", and finished the album. After listening to all the tunes, Shelby's staff came up with the album title, *For Women Only*, and also came up with the cover design, which was a puzzle to me then, and still is today. It was released in 1969, got some decent reviews, but sold only to my family.

Thirty-five years went by, and one day I got this voicemail from a guy in LA named Steve Stanley wanting to talk to me about re-releasing my album. I thought it was a joke. I was absolutely sure it was David Briggs up to another one of his pranks. But out of curiosity I returned the call, and after Steve asked a few questions, I began to realize this was not Briggs; it was for real.

We did a three-hour interview on the phone, Steve wrote the excellent, in-depth liner notes, and *For Women Only* was re-released in 2004 on an English label called Revola. It received many reviews, mostly positive, and was voted one of the twenty best reissues of 2004 in *Mojo Magazine*. Here are just a few of the reviews you will hopefully find interesting. This first review was actually written by the actor Jerry Orbach, who played Lennie Briscoe on the early *Law and Order* shows. He died that same year, probably from guilt for writing this review.

Creep Scanner

Friday, June 1, 2012

Bergen White-For Women Only

Jerry Orbach

If you have a penis, stop reading this post because Ol' Bergen clearly had a specific market in mind when he was recording this platter and it didn't include you. I'm almost afraid to post this here seeing as how I am one of the lesser sex. The only problem is that this spot ain't exactly all that happening with the ladies, barring one or two (hi Holly & Rachel). Okay, I guess some of us more effete dudes can get down with this too since it's actually quite a good album. Another dollar find that definitely is worth far more than the hundred pennies spent on it. Maybe us macs can use this is some trumped up seduction scenario. I just expect a lot of laughs from you special lady when you start pumping this through your stereo. It really should be titled "For Sad Aging Bastards Only," being as that's the only people who will probably give a shit about it anymore.

This review was from Jerry Orbach of "Law and Order" fame.

Right Place at the Write Time

BERGEN WHITE WOWS THE CRITICS!

Bergen White's Rev-Ola CD *For Women Only* managed to score 5 star reviews in last month's issues of both *Mojo* and *Uncut* magazine, an astounding feat which nobody can recall ever happening before. Bergen's version of David Gates' "Look At Me" from the CD is currently number six in *Mojo*'s top ten playlist.

We shouldn't really be surprised - it's a truly amazing record which deserves all the praise being heaped upon it. And, of course, the addition of several rare as hell bonus tracks and detailed liners with contributions from Bergen himself make it an even more essential and desirable package for all true lovers of classic late 60's/early 70's baroque pop.

Click here for more info and ordering details.

TOP TEN BEST SELLERS:

1. **Chuck & Mary Perrin**
The Last Word
CRREV 60
2. **Them**
Time Out! Time In For Them
CRREV 52
3. **Twin Engine**
CRREV 57
4. **Bergen White**
For Women Only
CRREV 56
5. **Triste Janero**
Meet Triste Janero
CRREV 43
6. **Euphoria**
A Gift From Euphoria
CRREV 55
7. **Belfast Gypsies**
Them Belfast Gypsies
CRREV 49
8. **October Country**
CRREV 51
9. **Liz Damon's Orient Express**
CRREV 40
10. **The Jazz Butcher's Free Lunch**
CRREV 54

JIMI HEY AKA DJ Keanu Reeves. Maybe this is inappropriate, but dang it if those beastiality websites don't violently arouse my vast imagination. I guess that's not really a bio per se but... oh shit. Here comes Karen. Look alive!

- **Animal Collective - Sung Tongs** Fuck! I wish these assholes would stop coming up with so many good ideas. I'm starting to feel inadequate. Fuckin' Avey Tits and Panda Bitch. Think you're all smart and shit. You probably have threesomes with manatees and polar bears wearing his and his matching Incredible String Band onesies. No. For reals. This album is a must own.
- **Bergen White - For Women Only** This is a gorgeous, lost classic, pop gem, obscure as ladybug lips, why wasn't this a hit, where the shit did it come from, string arrangements, elegant harmonies, type of thing. If you've been keeping up with Rev-ola's reissue roster, than you should own it, because it's one of the best ones yet. Bergen's moustache probably chaffed many pairs of thighs in his day. Chaffe on Bergen.
- **White Magic - Through the Sun Door EP** White Magic is Mira from Quixotic, and her homies Andy and Miggie. Together, they've made a sweet little record that totally stands out from the rest of the goober-esque shite that is normally shoved down our throats. I don't want to try and describe it cuz I'll make it sound less cool than it is. Does anyone else think Devendra Banhart needs to shut his stinking trap every once in a while? Cool it nature boy, I'm onto you.
- Buy the **Disco Inferno** reissues, because they were the most forward-thinking, underrated, most visionary band of the 90's, give or take a few others. The documentary "Stoked: The Mark 'Gator' Rogowski Story" is on DVD, and it's great. If you grew up in So Cal in the 80's and skated, you should definitely see this. It totally captures what a magic time it was to be a skater kid back then. Oh, and he kills a girl at the end. Not so cool, but the first half is a treat.
- **Aqua Teen Hunger Force DVD** I arrived at this later than everybody, but may Jehova strike me down if this isn't the funniest cartoon in the multiverse. I wish Meatwad was my roomate. He's so fucking cute. And what about Carl, the white trash neighbor? Hey Carl, don't worry buddy, she's on me, but you get the next round. Master Shake is the best asshole character ever. I love Aqua Teen.
- tip: If you're going to drink GHB, don't do it while working at Amoeba, or you will have to sit down in the breakroom for a while.

145

Finale

(There Will Be No More)

In the early '70s after I'd gotten my release from SSS International, I was signed to record some singles with Private Stock Records out of New York. They released three singles, one of which was "Duke of Earl". It was really doing well and had broken into the Top 100 in *Billboard Magazine*, so the dude who ran Private Stock, Larry Utah, flew to town to discuss our options. We had lunch at Maude's (that's where everybody who was anybody had lunch in those days, and they graciously let me in because they had seen me so many times with Beckham).

Larry wanted me to go on the road to promote "Duke of Earl". He wanted me to do *Midnight Special* with Wolfman Jack, *Hullabaloo*, *American Bandstand* with Dick Clark and *Solid Gold*, to mention a few. This was a big crossroads for me. Did I want to jeopardize my blossoming arranging career to pursue being a recording artist? As big a crossroads as it was, it took me about three seconds to make up my mind. I was not going on the road and lose the career I had built up as an arranger, so I told Larry no. He was quite upset to say the least, and asked, "Why the hell did you cut all this shit if you didn't want to be an artist?" A really good question I suppose, and my answer was not so good: "I just wanted to see if I could cut a hit record." He was not amused. Private Stock stopped all the promotion and the "Duke of Earl" disappeared from the charts. I also disappeared from the list of artists on Private Stock.

While all this was going on I had begun recording what would've been my follow-up to *For Women Only* with one of my favorite engineers, Charlie Tallent. He was running Jack Clement's studio, and we were recording all the stuff there. But when I was unceremoniously dumped from Private Stock, we sort of put everything on hold, since I no longer had a label. "On hold" lasted thirty-five years until 2010, when I decided I had too much good stuff to never release it. So I called on another of my favorite engineers, Tony Castle, to help me complete two more sides to finish out the CD. The two additional songs were one I wrote called "Curious to Know" and a Dennis Linde classic called "Lookout Mountain".

Tony remixed as much as was possible, considering the first eight songs had already been mixed thirty-five years earlier. He was extremely limited as to what he could do, but he did a hell of a job making these tunes feel alive again. In 2010 I released it myself on CD Baby, an online distributer of independent music. I really meant what I said in the title of this chapter. *Finale*. There will be no more!

That's all I got, baby.

Anne Murray and me, In Toronto recording her duet with Glen Campbell on Glen's album "Show Me Your Way" in 1991.

Me, Jimmy Webb and Glen Campbell at Creative Recording working on "The Four Horseman" in 1991.

Dave Loggins, me and Yvonne Hodges doing background vocals on Jerry Lee Lewis for Jerry Kennedy in 1978.

Wayne Newton with my niece Kellye and my mother at Eleven Eleven Sound in late '80s.

MaraBeth Quin, Jon Mark Ivey, Kira Small and me at the Chicago Theatre in 2013.

Buzz Cason, Carol Montgomery, Mary Holliday and me doing backgrounds for Bob Dylan at Columbia Studios in the mid '70s.

Me conducting at Ocean Way Studio for Ray Price in 2012.

Me, Marijohn Wilkin and Archie Campbell doing the Syndicated Grand Ole Opry Show from the Ryman in 1966.

Me looking cool at Versailles Apartments in 1974.

Shane McConnell, Garth and me after a background vocal session in 2012.

Mark Ivey, Garth, Kira Small, Lisa Silver and me at Allentown Studio after doing backgrounds for Garth in 2010.

Me, Glen Campbell and Jimmy Webb at Creative Recording in 1991 recording the "Show Me Your Way" LP.

Greg Forsman, Greg Herrington and Glen Snow. 75% of Martina's band at the Symphony Center in 2018.

Paul Worley, Mark Ivey, Chris Isacc, me, Shane McConnell and Wes Hightower working on Chris Isaac's CD in 2015 called "First Comes the Night".

Martina, MaraBeth Quin, Kira Small, Mark Ivey and me. The "Joy of Christmas" show in Pittsburgh in 2013.

Me conducting. Adding strings to a Jon Secada CD at Ocean Way Studio in 2010.

The Marijohn Singers (me, Marijohn Wilkin, Glenn Baxter, Ed Bruce), George Morgan, unknown, Archie Campbell, Dolly, Speck Rhodes, Grandpa Jones, Porter Wagoner, Ramona and Buck Trent. Performing at the Grand Ole Opry at the Ryman in 1966.

From left, Kyle Lehning and wife Cynthia, me, Lisa Silver, Clayton Ivey, Sheri Huffman and Diane Vanette. Dinner with the Cherry Sisters at the 360 Bistro in 2018.

My hands. Reid Shippen took this photo at his studio while I was writing down his ideas for "Here Come the Mummy's" in 2014.

Larry Hall, me, Lionel Cartwright and Kyle Lehning.

In 2015 at New Hope Auditorium recording the ambience for Randy Travis CD called "This Never Happened". It really didn't!

Just inside the back door is Joe Babcock, four to five gals I'm sure including Ricky Page and Delores Edgin, Hurshel Wiginton, Gordon Stoker, me, Neal Mathews shouting in my left ear, Hoyt Hawkins, Hank Levine sitting on a stool, long time Columbia employee Ed Hubbard behind the horn section, Harold Bradley, Mark Morris, Ben Keith on steel, Norm Ray, Steve Sefsik, Johnny Duke, the back of Dennis Good's head, Shelley Kurland, Lillian Hunt, Carl Gorodetsky, Pam Sixfin and many more that are unidentifiable. A big rehearsal for something at Columbia Studio "B" in the mid 70's.

Seated on the left and coming forward is Grady Martin, Fred Carter Jr., Pete Drake, Wayne Moss' back with Charlie McCoy to his right then George Hamilton IV, standing from left is Henry Strzelecki, Norro Wilson, Buzz Cason and myself. In the background is Hargis "Pig" Robbins at the piano. At a George Hamilton IV session at RCA produced by Bob Ferguson in 1973.

Standing from left Joe Talbot, Bob Beckham, Randy Goodrum, unknown, Walter Sills, Fred Kewley, unknown, unknown, Pat Bergeson, Roger Sovine, Ray Baker and me. Seated from left: Eddy Arnold, Owen Bradley, Chet Atkins, Harry Warner, Billy Edd Wheeler and Ray Stevens. Beckham's surprise birthday party for Chet at Valentino's in 1985.

A man and his women.

*Left to right: Tania Hancheroff, Lisa Silver,
me and Kira Small recording background vocals on Randy Travis'
Christmas LP with Kyle Lehning producing in 2021.*

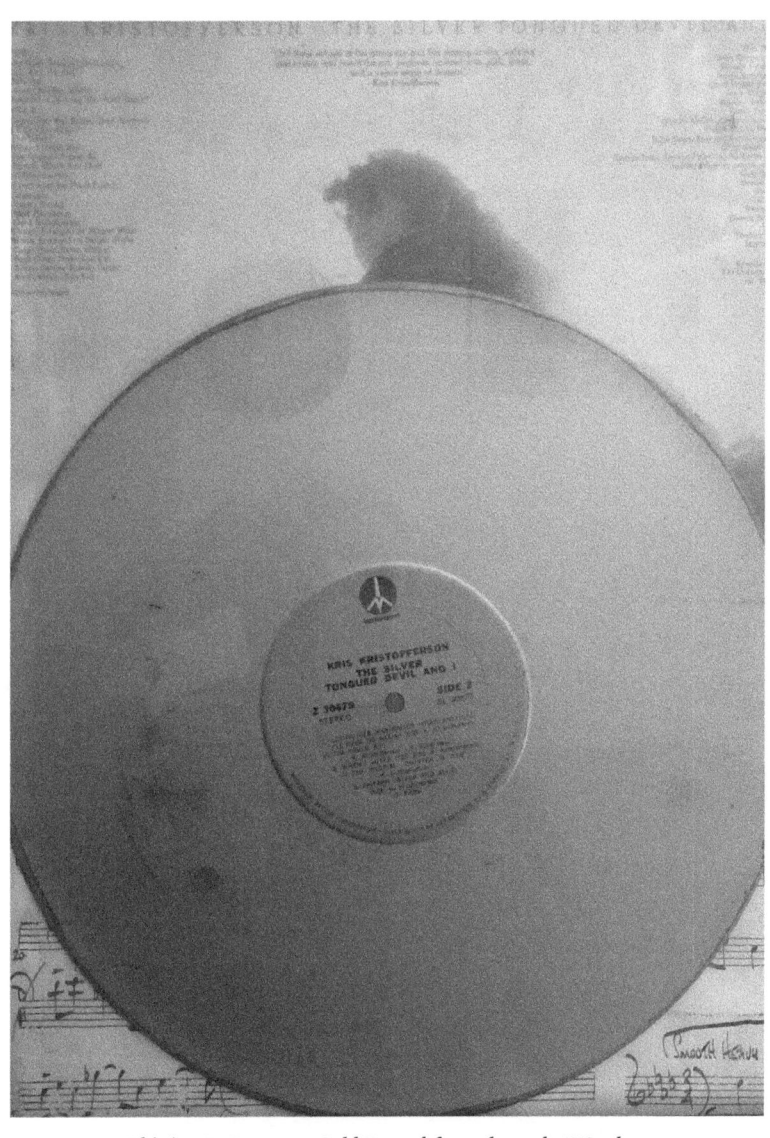

*This is MY Damnass Gold Record from the early '70s that
I mentioned in Fred Foster's chapter.*